Collins
New
Primary
Maths

Differentiation Pack 5

Series Editor: Peter Clarke

Authors: Jeanette Mumford, Sandra Roberts, Andrew Edmondson

William Collins' dream of knowledge for all began with the publication of his first book in 1819. A self-educated mill worker, he not only enriched millions of lives, but also founded a flourishing publishing house. Today, staying true to this spirit, Collins books are packed with inspiration, innovation and practical expertise. They place you at the centre of a world of possibility and give you exactly what you need to explore it.

Collins. Freedom to teach.

Published by Collins
An imprint of HarperCollinsPublishers
77 – 85 Fulham Palace Road
Hammersmith
London
W6 8JB

Browse the complete Collins catalogue at
www.collinseducation.com

© HarperCollinsPublishers Limited 2008

10 9 8 7 6 5 4

ISBN-13 978-0-00-722041-0

British Library Cataloguing in Publication Data
A Catalogue record for this publication is available from the British Library

Cover design by Laing&Carroll
Cover artwork by Jonatronix Ltd
Internal design by Mark Walker and Steve Evans Design
Illustrations by Mark Walker and Steve Evans
Edited by Jean Rustean
Proofread by Ros Davies

Printed and bound by Martins the Printers, Berwick-upon-Tweed

Contents

Contents

Contents

Contents

Unit A3

Unit B3

Unit C3

Contents

Name _____ Date _____

Fractions and decimals

● **Explain what each digit represents in whole numbers and decimals up to one place**

This stick is divided into ten parts. Each part is a tenth.

1 Write the tenths as fractions and then as decimals

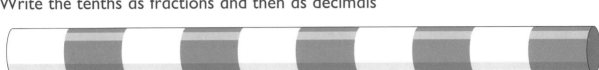

Fractions

$\frac{1}{10}$		$\frac{3}{10}$							

Decimals

0·1		0·3							

2 Write the decimal that goes with each of these fractions.

a $\frac{3}{10}$ = $\boxed{0·3}$ **b** $\frac{6}{10}$ = ☐   **c** $\frac{5}{10}$ = ☐

d $\frac{1}{10}$ = ☐   **e** $\frac{4}{10}$ = ☐   **f** $\frac{7}{10}$ = ☐

g $\frac{8}{10}$ = ☐   **h** $\frac{2}{10}$ = ☐   **i** $\frac{9}{10}$ = ☐

Name _____ Date _____

Working it out mentally

● Add or subtract any pair of two-digit numbers mentally

1 Work out these calculations adding the tens and then the units.

a 48 + 26 = | 74 |
40 + 20 = | 60 |
8 + 6 = | 14 |

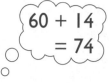 60 + 14 = 74

b 35 + 64 = ☐
30 + 60 = ☐
5 + 4 = ☐

c 71 + 46 = ☐
70 + 40 = ☐
1 + 6 = ☐

d 53 + 28 = ☐
50 + 20 = ☐
3 + 8 = ☐

e 43 + 59 = ☐
40 + 50 = ☐
3 + 9 = ☐

f 84 + 57 = ☐
80 + 50 = ☐
4 + 7 = ☐

g 85 + 61 = ☐
80 + 60 = ☐
5 + 1 = ☐

h 17 + 69 = ☐
10 + 60 = ☐
7 + 9 = ☐

2 Find the difference between these numbers using the empty number line.

a 68 – 29 =   (1, 30, 8) 29 30 60 68 | 39 |

b 79 – 37 =   37 ─── 79   ☐

c 88 – 49 =   49 ─── 88   ☐

d 104 – 97 =   97 ─── 104   ☐

e 102 – 98 =   98 ─── 102   ☐

f 105 – 96 =   96 ─── 105   ☐

g 207 – 199 =   199 ─── 207   ☐

Name _____ Date _____

Number sequences

● **Recognise and extend number sequences**

1 Continue the number sequences.

a   4   11   18   ☐   ☐   ☐   ☐

b   23   15   7   ☐   ☐   ☐   ☐   ☐

c   −13   −8   −3   ☐   ☐   ☐   ☐

d   36   47   58   ☐   ☐   ☐   ☐

2 Write the missing numbers in these number sequences.

a   29   24   ☐   ☐   ☐   4   −1   ☐

b   11   ☐   ☐   35   43   ☐   59

c   ☐   −3   6   ☐   24   ☐   ☐

d   38   50   ☐   ☐   86   98   ☐   ☐

3 Choose two of the numbers on the right and write a sequence that has your numbers in it. Choose other numbers. How many different sequences can you make?

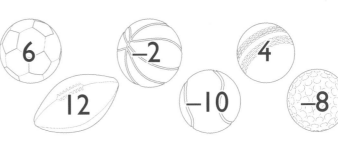

6   −2   4   12   −10   −8

Collins New Primary Maths   © HarperCollinsPublishers Ltd 2008

Name _____ Date _____

Multiplication

● **Multiply a two-digit number by a one-digit number**

For each calculation, approximate the answer first, then use the grid to work out the answer. Show all your working.

a   64 × 4   ○○

×	60	4
4		

=

b   97 × 3   ○○

×	90	7
3		

=

c   51 × 6   ○○

×	50	1
6		

=

d   82 × 3   ○○

×	80	2
3		

=

e   33 × 7   ○○

×	30	3
7		

=

f   78 × 5   ○○

×	70	8
5		

=

g   23 × 8   ○○

×	20	3
8		

=

h   34 × 9   ○○

×	30	4
9		

=

i   52 × 6   ○○

×	50	2
6		

=

© Collins
New
Primary
Maths

Name _____ Date _____

Ordering whole numbers

● **Order whole numbers**

1 Make up ten 5-digit numbers using each of these digits. Write them in the first grid. Put them in order, from smallest to largest, in the second grid.

90 768	

2 Choose two of your numbers and write them in words.

....

....

3 Write the number in the box that comes about halfway between each pair of numbers.

a 45 899 [   ] 48 658

b 71 263 [   ] 74 598

c 86 187 [   ] 93 210

d 94 523 [   ] 94 820

e 81 301 [   ] 87 398

Name _____ Date _____

Missing digits

● **Use efficient written methods to add whole numbers**

Work out the missing digits from these calculations.

Remember to allow for numbers that have been carried.

a
```
 3 7 6 8
+  5 6 5
─────────
 4 3 3 3
```

b
```
 2 9 ⬡ 2
+  3 6 9
─────────
 3 ⬡ 3 1
```

c
```
 3 ⬡ 7 8
+  9 4 6
─────────
 ⬡ 0 2 4
```

d
```
 ⬡ 7 6 2
+  5 7 ⬡
─────────
 5 3 4 1
```

e
```
 4 ⬡ 5 7
+  7 8 ⬡
─────────
 5 3 4 0
```

f
```
 5 8 9 2
+ ⬡ 7 8
─────────
 6 1 ⬡ 0
```

g
```
 ⬡ 6 5 7
+  4 8 4
─────────
 5 1 4 ⬡
```

h
```
 3 4 9 6
+  5 ⬡ 7
─────────
 4 0 9 ⬡
```

i
```
 ⬡ 3 5 ⬡
+  8 7 5
─────────
 5 2 3 3
```

j
```
 ⬡ 8 0 8
+  6 9 7
─────────
 6 5 0 ⬡
```

k
```
 3 6 8 2
+ ⬡ 5 7 1
─────────
 6 2 ⬡ 3
```

l
```
 4 3 8 3
+ 1 ⬡ 4 5
─────────
 6 1 2 ⬡
```

m
```
 6 ⬡ 2 8
+ 2 6 4 9
─────────
 9 4 ⬡ 7
```

n
```
 ⬡ 4 6 2
+ 2 9 3 ⬡
─────────
 8 3 9 9
```

o
```
 3 6 5 ⬡
+ 3 7 8 9
─────────
 7 ⬡ 4 1
```

Collins
New
Primary
Maths

Name _____ Date _____

Number sequences

● **Recognise and extend number sequences**

1 Fill in the missing numbers in each sequence.
Write the rule in the box.

a 12, 23, 34, _____, _____, _____, _____, _____, _____, _____. ☐

b 91, _____, _____, 97, _____, _____, 103, 105, _____, _____. ☐

c 25, 16, 7, _____, _____, _____, _____, _____, _____, _____. ☐

d 30, 34, 38, _____, _____, _____, _____, _____, _____, _____. ☐

e −15, −11, _____, −3, _____, _____, _____, _____, _____, _____. ☐

f −96, _____, _____, _____, _____, _____, _____, −26, _____, −6. ☐

2 Choose a starting number and write it in the oval.
Then fill in the missing numbers by following the rules given.

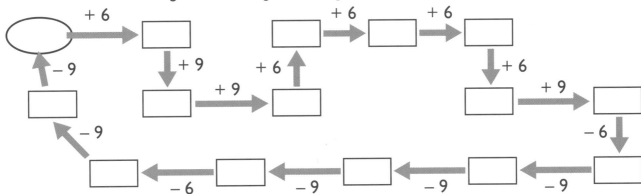

3 Write a number sequence that includes the number −4.

What is the rule? ☐

4 Write a number sequence that includes the number −9.

☐ → ☐ → ☐ → ☐ → ☐ → ☐ → ☐

What is the rule? ☐

Collins
New
Primary
Maths

Name _____ Date _____

Multiplication

● **Multiply a two-digit or three-digit number by a one-digit number**

For each calculation, approximate the answer first, then work out the answer. Show all your working.

a 87 × 4 ∘∘○

b 76 × 6 ∘∘○

c 93 × 7 ∘∘○

d 64 × 9 ∘∘○

e 124 × 3 ∘∘○

f 285 × 4 ∘∘○

g 147 × 7 ∘∘○

h 218 × 6 ∘∘○

i 184 × 8 ∘∘○

Collins
New
Primary
Maths

Name _____ Date _____

Money subtraction

● **Use an efficient method to subtract decimals**

1 Subtract these amounts from each other. Remember when
   subtracting using this method, the decimal points must be underneath each other.

a

£	4	·	6	7
− £	2	·	3	1
		·		

b

£	8	·	7	2
− £	5	·	6	1
		·		

c

£	6	·	3	5
− £	3	·	1	2
		·		

d

£	9	·	6	2
− £	5	·	1	0
		·		

e

£	7	·	5	4
− £		·	3	2

f

£	9	·	6	1
− £	2	·	3	4
		·		

g

£	6	·	7	3
− £	4	·	3	5
		·		

h

X25
card – cream.

		·	5	1
		·	5	1
		·		

j

£	7	·	7	4
− £	4	·	2	8
		·		

k

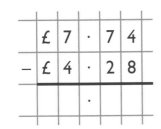

	9	·	3	2
	4	·	8	6
		·		

2 Write these calculations out yourself. Then work them out.

a £ 8·32 − £ 3·90

b £ 7·52 − £ 2·81

c £ 8·16 − £ 5·92

d £ 9·95 − £ 2·93

Collins
New
Primary
Maths

Name _____ Date _____

Make the set

- Explore patterns, properties and relationships and propose a general statement involving numbers; identify examples for which the statement is true or false

Look at the numbers in the sets. Write down the rule and write in four more numbers

1 14, 36, 8, 44, 60, 28, 72, ... , ... , ... , ...

rule

2 30, 100, 20, 50, 160, 200, ... , ... , ... , ...

rule

3 6, 12, 21, 3, 30, ... , ... , ... , ...

rule

4 11, 27, 35, 63, 99, ... , ... , ... , ...

rule

5 Make up two sets of your own. Write down what the rule is.

.... , ... , ... , ... , ... , ... , ... , ...

rule

.... , ... , ... , ... , ... , ... , ... , ...

rule

Collins
New
Primary
Maths

Name _____ Date _____

Find-a-fact game

● **Recall multiplication facts up to 10 × 10 and derive quickly the related division facts**

A game for 2–3 players.

● Cover each number fact with a counter.

● Take turns to uncover a fact and give the answer. If the answer is correct, keep the counter.

You need:

● 36 large counters

● The player with the most counters at the end is the winner.

6 × 8	14 ÷ 2	8 × 9	27 ÷ 9	8 × 4	9 × 9
15 ÷ 5	5 × 6	18 ÷ 2	6 × 4	5 ÷ 0	10 × 10
7 × 7	36 ÷ 4	8 × 2	56 ÷ 7	6 × 6	4 × 7
9 × 5	28 ÷ 7	40 ÷ 5	7 × 3	24 ÷ 3	10 ÷ 2
8 × 0	42 ÷ 6	7 × 5	48 ÷ 8	9 × 6	63 ÷ 9
12 ÷ 1	2 × 9	90 ÷ 10	8 × 8	18 ÷ 6	9 × 3

Name _____ Date _____

Finding factors

● **Find all the pairs of factors of any number up to 100**

1 Write two multiplication number
   sentences for each set of numbers.

   Decide which numbers are the
   factors and which number is the product.

   Circle the product in each set.

a
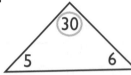

$5 \times 6 = 30$
$6 \times 5 = 30$

b
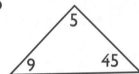

c

d
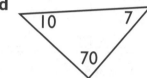

e
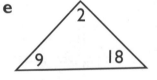

f
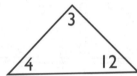

g

h
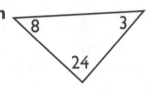

2 Write all of the factors for each number by writing out each pair in order.

9   12   16   24   18

Collins
New
Primary
Maths

Name _____ Date _____

Identifying nets

● **Identify different nets for an open cube**

1 Predict which of these shapes are nets and will form an open cube. Record in the table.

You need:
● scissors

2 Carefully cut out the shapes along the dashed (----) lines. Fold up each shape along the dotted (·······) lines to find which are nets for open boxes. Put a ✓ in the Check column if your prediction is correct.

Shape	Is a net	Is not a net	Check
a			
b			
c			
d			
e			
f			

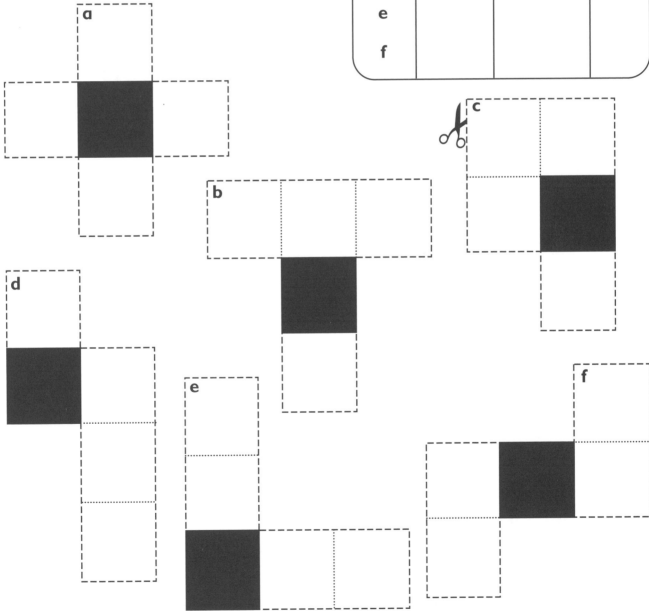

Name _____ Date _____

Drawing diagonals

● Recognise and explain patterns and relationships
in 2-D shapes

A diagonal of a polygon is a straight line
joining any two vertices not next to each
other.

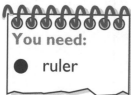

You need:
● ruler

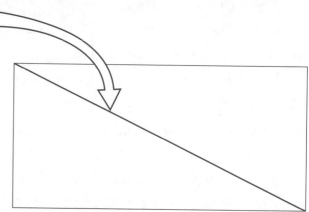

Draw all the diagonals in these quadrilaterals.

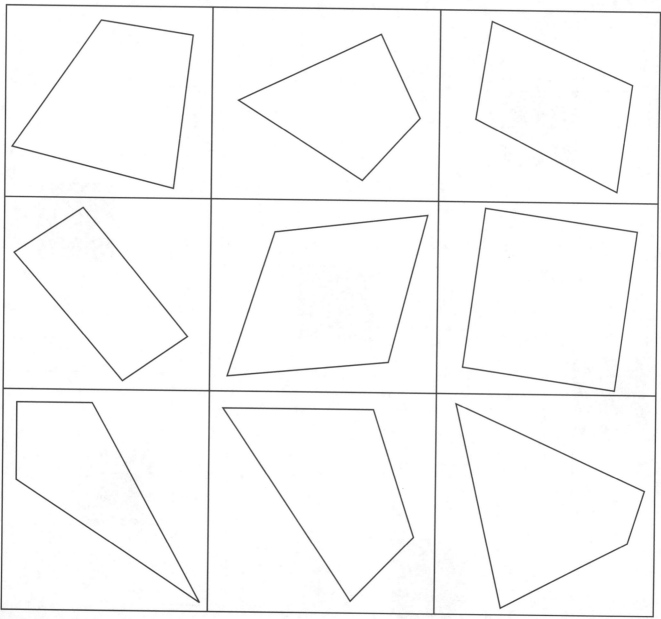

Collins
New
Primary
Maths

Name _____ Date _____

Put back what you borrow

● **Use efficient methods to subtract whole numbers**

These calculations have been worked out, but they have been copied without the borrowing. Work out where the borrowing should be.

a
```
  ³1 ³1
 4 6 4 2
-  7 2 5
 3 9 1 7
```

b
```
 5 2 6 5
-   8 8 2
 4 3 8 3
```

c
```
 6 1 2 7
-   5 6 4
 5 5 6 3
```

d
```
 5 4 0 7
-   6 3 2
 4 7 7 5
```

e
```
 7 2 9 2
-   6 4 8
 6 6 4 4
```

f
```
 6 6 7 2
-   8 3 5
 5 8 3 7
```

g
```
 5 3 8 1
-   5 4 5
 4 8 3 6
```

h
```
 4 5 0 3
-   9 6 1
 3 5 4 2
```

i
```
 8 2 2 7
-   7 7 3
 7 4 5 4
```

j
```
 9 1 5 7
-   3 9 1
 8 7 6 6
```

k
```
 7 0 8 3
-   6 2 7
 6 4 5 6
```

l
```
 6 3 9 2
-   7 8 5
 5 6 0 7
```

m
```
 5 7 2 3
-   9 7 5
 4 7 4 8
```

n
```
 9 3 4 0
-   8 6 3
 8 4 7 7
```

o
```
 8 2 1 5
-   7 4 9
 7 4 6 6
```

Name _____ Date _____

What's missing?

- **Use an efficient written method to add decimals**

Find the missing numbers in these calculations.

a
```
    4 7 . ▓
  + 3 9 . 1
  ─────────
    8 6 . 9
```

b
```
      2 . 7 6
  + ▓ . 1 2
  ─────────
  1 1 . 8 8
```

c
```
    6 . 3 4
  + 2 . ▓ 7
  ─────────
    8 . 5 1
```

d
```
    7 3 . ▓
  + 2 1 . 9
  ─────────
    9 5 . 5
```

e
```
    ▓ 2 . 8
  + 3 8 . 1
  ─────────
  1 0 0 . 9
```

f
```
    2 . 9 ▓
  + 7 . 0 6
  ─────────
  1 0 . 0 2
```

g
```
    ▓ . 6 ▓
  + 2 . 9 6
  ─────────
    7 . 6 3
```

h
```
    ▓ 1 . 7
  + 2 1 . ▓
  ─────────
  1 0 3 . 4
```

i
```
    5 7 . ▓
  + 1 ▓ . 8
  ─────────
    7 4 . 0
```

j
```
    9 . ▓ 3
  + ▓ . 2 8
  ─────────
  1 3 . 3 1
```

k
```
    ▓ 8 . 4
  + 5 6 . ▓
  ─────────
    9 4 . 6
```

l
```
    4 2 . ▓
  + 6 ▓ . 7
  ─────────
  1 0 8 . 6
```

m
```
    6 . 8 ▓
  + ▓ . 6 1
  ─────────
  1 4 . 4 8
```

n
```
    4 . 9 ▓
  + ▓ . 2 4
  ─────────
  1 3 . 2 0
```

o
```
    ▓ 7 . 5
  + 3 8 . ▓
  ─────────
  1 2 6 . 1
```

Collins New Primary Maths

Name _____   Date _____

Cross-number puzzle

- **Recall multiplication facts up to 10 × 10 and derive quickly the related division facts**

Fill in the blank squares using numbers or the operations × or ÷.

	÷	8	=	6		18		9	=	2		
÷		×		×		÷			×			
	÷		=			3	×		=			42
=		=		=		=		×		=		÷
4		24						9		24		7
					20			=				
					÷				÷	6	=	
			5	×		=	25					
60					=			8	×	6	=	
		×			4			×		=		÷
10	÷	1	=							1		4
=		=						=				=
6	×		=	54				72	÷		=	

Collins New Primary Maths

Name _____ Date _____

Finding factors

● **Find all the pairs of factors of any number up to 100**

1   Colour the factors for each number.

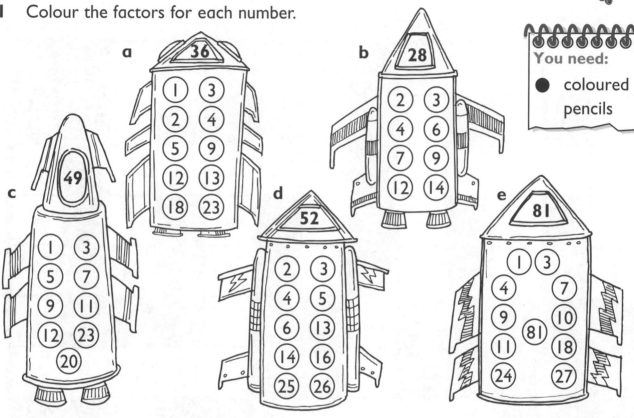

You need:
● coloured pencils

2   Write all of the factors for each number by working out each pair in order.

a	b	c	d	e
56	72	96	48	64

3   Is the smaller number a factor of the larger number?
Colour the smaller number if it is, cross it out if it is not.

a	b	c	d	e	f
5 92	7 63	4 76	8 144	10 150	6 84

g	h	i	j	k	l
13 117	9 156	14 168	18 72	15 270	25 375

© Collins
New
Primary
Maths

Name _____ Date _____

Designing nets

● **Identify different nets for an open cube**

This open cube has a black stripe all the way round.

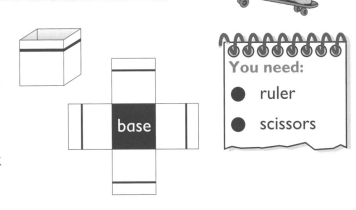

You need:
● ruler
● scissors

1 Decide where the black stripes go on each of these nets. Draw them using a ruler.

2 Cut out and fold up each net to check if the black stripe is at the same level all the way round each cube.

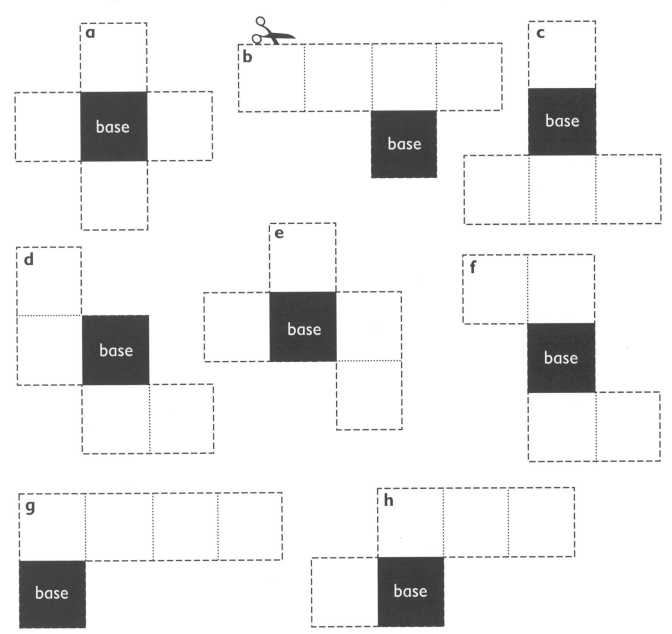

Collins New Primary Maths

Name _____ Date _____

More diagonals

● Recognise and explain patterns and relationships in 2-D shapes, generalise and predict

a Draw all the diagonals in these regular polygons.

You need:
● ruler

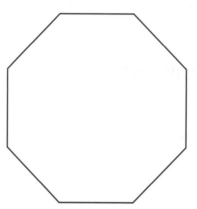

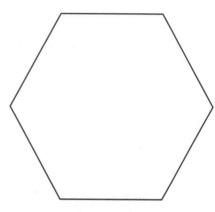

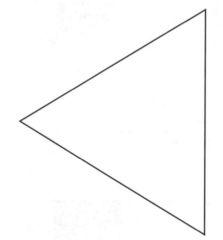

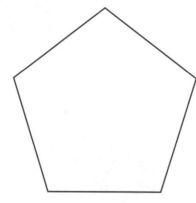

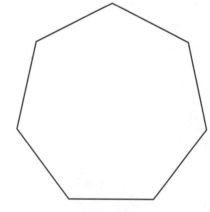

b Complete this table.

Number of sides	3	4	5	6	7	8
Number of diagonals						

c Predict the number of diagonals for a 9-sided shape.

Use the other side of this sheet to check your prediction.

Collins New Primary Maths

Name _____ Date _____

Lines in circles

- **Measure and draw lines to the nearest millimetre**

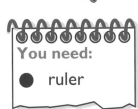

1 a Join these points with straight lines.
      1 to 2, 1 to 3, 1 to 4 and 1 to 5.

  b Measure each line to the nearest
      millimetre. Complete the table.

HINT
Measure from
dot centre to dot
centre

You need:
- ruler

Line	Length in mm
1 to 2	48 mm
1 to 3	
1 to 4	
1 to 5	

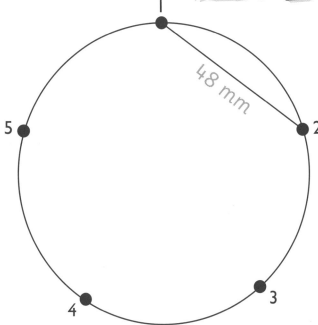

2 a Join these points. Measure each line
      to the nearest mm.

2 to 4 [   ] mm

4 to 6 [   ] mm

6 to 2 [   ] mm

b Write what you notice
    about the lengths.

[   ]

c Join and measure the distance
    between these points.

2 to 3 [   ] mm

2 to 5 [   ] mm

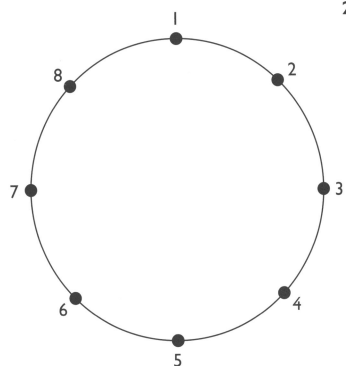

Collins
New
Primary
Maths

Name _____ Date _____

Breakfast

● **Collect, organise and present data**

Andy took these orders for breakfast.

sausages ✓ eggs ✓ toast beans	toast beans eggs	mushrooms beans	sausages eggs toast beans	beans eggs mushrooms
beans toast eggs	eggs sausages toast	toast eggs	eggs sausages mushrooms beans	beans eggs sausages

1 Tick each portion and make a tally mark in the chart alongside.

2 Add up the tally marks and write down the total number of each type of food.

Food	Tally	Total
sausages		
eggs		
toast		
mushrooms		
beans		

3 Use the information presented in the table above to answer these questions:

a How many people ordered mushrooms? ☐

b What is the most popular breakfast food? ☐

c What is the least popular breakfast food? ☐

4 Now use the information from the table to complete the bar chart.

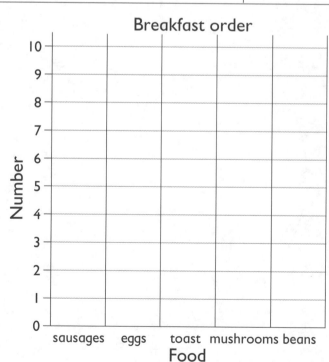

© HarperCollins*Publishers* Ltd 2008

Name _____ Date _____

More modes

● **Find the mode of a set of data**

1   Find the mode of these letters.

   a T, T, P, R, N

   b A, A, A, B, C, C

   c E, E, I, O, O, O, U, U

   d P, C, B, C, P, U, P

2   Find the two modes of these letters.

   a R, S, S, T, U, U

   b K, K, L, L, L, M, M, O, O, O

   c T, T, D, E, E, O, U

   d N, M, R, M, T, N

3   Find the mode of these numbers.

   a 6, 9, 10, 15, 15

   b 8, 8, 8, 4, 4, 3, 3

   c 20, 10, 30, 20

   d 5, 8, 9, 5, 8, 5

4   Find the two modes of these numbers.

   a 1, 2, 2, 3, 5, 5

   b 50, 50, 100, 100, 200

   c 6, 3, 3, 4, 6, 3, 6

   d 0, 10, 10, 0, 20, 10, 0

5   Find the mode or modes.

   a D, F, D, E, F, D

   b M, N, T, A, M, A

   c 50, 20, 20, 40, 30, 40, 20

   d 3, 2, 1, 3, 1, 2, 1, 3

6   Roll a 1-6 dice 30 times.

Each time you roll the dice, place a tally mark in Table 1 and record the number you rolled in Table 2.

You need:
● 1-6 dice

Table 1

Tally	Total number of times dice is rolled
	30

What is the mode?

Table 2

Number	Tally	Number
1		
2		
3		
4		
5		
6		

7   If you rolled a 1–6 dice another 30 times, would you get the same mode?

Roll the dice again to find out. Record your results on the back of this sheet.

Name _____ Date _____

Fruit portions

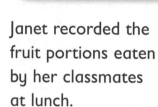

● **Collect and organise data to answer a question**

Janet recorded the fruit portions eaten by her classmates at lunch.

apple orange pear banana peach apple banana Kiwi banana apple orange
banana apple plum banana apple banana peach orange pear peach peach
peach plum orange plum banana orange apple Kiwi apple pear orange
banana apple orange banana pear banana apple banana banana

1 Make a tally mark for each fruit.

2 Add up the tally marks and write down the totals.

3 Use the information in the table to answer these questions.

Fruit	Tally	Total
apple		
banana		
kiwi		
orange		
peach		
pear		
plum		

a Which was the most popular fruit (the mode)? _____

b Which was the least popular fruit? _____

c Did more children eat apples or oranges? _____ How many more? _____

d Which type of fruit did 4 children have for lunch? _____

4 Complete the bar chart below.

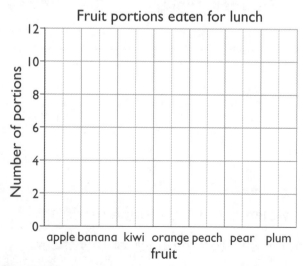

Fruit portions eaten for lunch

Number of portions — fruit (apple, banana, kiwi, orange, peach, pear, plum)

5 Complete the pictogram below.

apple	
banana	
kiwi	
orange	
peach	
pear	
plum	

Collins New Primary Maths

Name _____ Date _____

Patterns with millimetres

● **Measure and draw lines to the nearest millimetre**

1 a Join the points to make a pattern. Join 1 to 1, 2 to 2, 3 to 3 and so on.

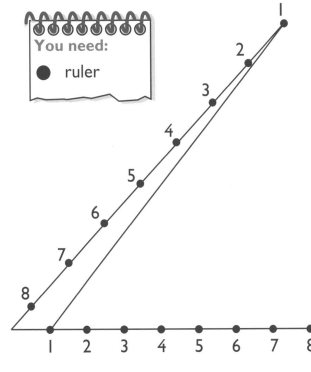

You need:
● ruler

b Measure the lines to the nearest millimetre. Complete this table.

Line	To the nearest mm
1 to 1	
2 to 2	
3 to 3	
4 to 4	
5 to 5	
6 to 6	
7 to 7	
8 to 8	

2 a Using the same method, join the points around the square – but don't join points on opposite sides of the square.

b Measure these lines:

1 to 1	mm
2 to 2	mm
3 to 3	mm
4 to 4	mm
5 to 5	mm
6 to 6	mm
7 to 7	mm

c Write what you notice about the lengths.

© HarperCollins*Publishers* Ltd 2008

Collins
New
Primary
Maths

Name _____ Date _____

Sandwich bar

- ● Compare bar charts

The bar chart shows the number of brown bread sandwiches that were sold at a sandwich bar.

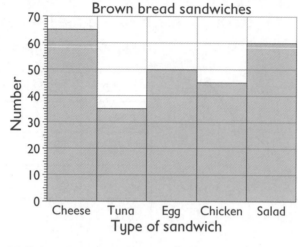

Brown bread sandwiches

1   Copy and complete the table.

Brown bread sandwiches

Sandwich	Number
Cheese	
Tuna	
Egg	
Chicken	
Salad	

The table on the right shows the white bread sandwiches sold.

White bread sandwiches

Sandwich	Number
Cheese	52
Tuna	73
Egg	32
Chicken	51
Salad	45

2   Copy and complete the bar chart.

White bread sandwiches

3   Pu Wai says, 'People who eat brown bread sandwiches eat more vegetarian food.'

Compare the bar charts. Do you think Pu Wai is right? Explain your answer.

You need:
- ● 1 cm squared paper
- ● graph paper   ● ruler

4   Using graph paper, draw the bar chart for white bread sandwiches again. This time use the scale shown here.

Which bar chart do you think is most useful? Explain your answer.

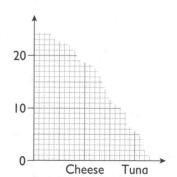

Collins
New
Primary
Maths

Name _____ Date _____

Island bird bar charts

● **Use graphs to explain answers to questions**

1 The bar line chart shows the birds that visited an island in spring.

Copy and complete the table.

Bird	Number visiting

You need:
● graph paper
● ruler

2 The table below shows the birds that left the island in autumn.

Bird	Number leaving
wagtail	90
redstart	160
sandpiper	124
reed warbler	72
flycatcher	48
wheatear	100
dunlin	116

Draw a bar line chart using graph paper.

3 **a** How many sandpipers visited in spring? ☐

b How many flycatchers left in autumn? ☐

c What is the most popular (mode) bird visiting in spring?
☐

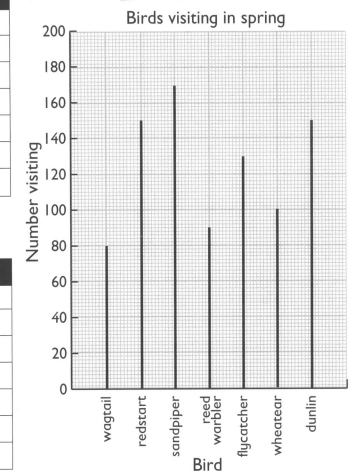

Birds visiting in spring

d What is the mode for birds leaving in autumn?
☐

e How many birds arrived in spring altogether? ☐

f Did more or fewer birds leave in autumn than arrived in spring?
☐

How many more or fewer? ☐

Name _____ Date _____

Tracks

● Construct pictograms, bar chart and bar line charts to represent the frequencies of events

The bar line chart shows the sizes of some mp3 files for music tracks. They have been rounded up to the nearest megabyte (MB).

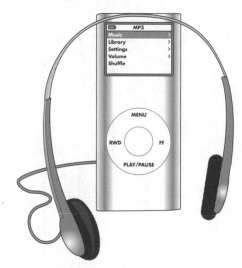

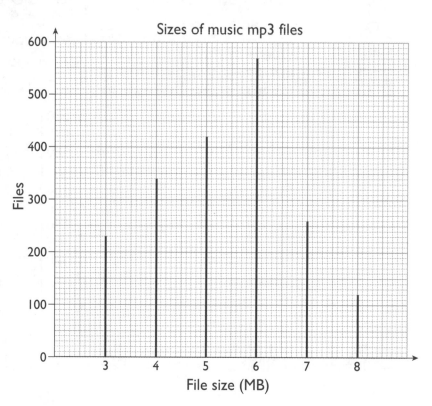

Sizes of music mp3 files

1   **a** What is the mode?

   b How many files are 4 MB?

   c How many files are smaller than the mode?

2   Draw a pictogram for the data.

    = 100 MB

3   Draw a bar chart for the data.

4   **a** Use a tally chart to record the lengths, in minutes, of 50 music tracks from CDs. They must be between 3 and 10 minutes. Round up their sizes to the nearest minute first.

   b Draw a chart for the data.

You need:

● graph paper   ● ruler

Collins
New
Primary
Maths

Name _____ Date _____

Family holiday

● **Solve word problems involving one or more steps**

Prices

ADULT: £18
CHILD: £4

ADULT: £223
CHILD: £132

Cost per day:
£145

ADULT: £15
CHILD: £10
(per week)

Plan a holiday for your family. Read the word problems.
Choose an appropriate method of
calculating your answer:

● mental

● mental with jottings

● paper and pencil

a How much does it cost your family to travel on the train to the airport?	**b** What is the total cost of insurance for your family for a week?	**c** How much are the flights for your parent(s)? How much are the flights for the children? What is the total cost?
d You go on holiday for 7 days. How much does the accommodation cost? How much more does it cost to stay for 10 days?	**e** When you return from your holiday, train fares have risen by £1 for adults and 50p for children. How much does it cost you to travel home by train?	**f** What is the total cost of your 7 day holiday?

Name _____ Date _____

Perimeter game

- **Understand, measure and calculate perimeters of rectangles and regular polygons**

A game for two players.

You need:

- about 12 2-D shapes in different sizes ● ruler

Instructions

Player A

● Choose a shape.

Player B

● Estimate the perimeter of Player A's shape and record in centimetres.

● Measure the perimeter to the nearest centimetre.

● Ask Player A to check your answer.

● Record the measured perimeter.

● Work out the difference between estimate and measure.

● Write your score in the table.

● Now choose a shape for Player A to estimate.

The player with the higher score is the winner.

Scoring

To within 1 cm: 3 points

To within 2 cm: 2 points

To within 3 cm: 1 point

Player A

Length of perimeter		Score
Estimate	Measure	

Player B

Length of perimeter		Score
Estimate	Measure	

Collins New Primary Maths

Name _____ Date _____

Watches and clocks

● **Read the time on a 24-hour digital clock and use 24-hour notation**

1 Fill in the missing hours on this 24-hour clock.

2 Fill in the missing times on these different clocks. The first row has been done for you.

wall clock analogue	a.m. or p.m.	watch 12-hour digital	video recorder 24-hour digital
a	pm	4 : 00	16 : 00
b	am		:
c	am	11 : 15	:
d	pm	3 : 45	:
e			21 : 10
f			14 : 40
g			08 : 45

Name _____ Date _____

On target

- **Read and plot co-ordinates**

A game for two players.

- Take turns to roll the dice.

- Put a counter on the co-ordinates shown by the dice.

- If the co-ordinate is already covered by your opponent's counter, you miss a turn.

- If the co-ordinate is already covered by one of your counters, roll the dice again.

- The game stops when one player has placed all 10 counters.

- Add up your points. The player with more points is the winner.

You need:

- 10 small counters in one colour (per player)

- 2 × 1-6 dice in different colours, one colour for the x-axis and one for the y-axis

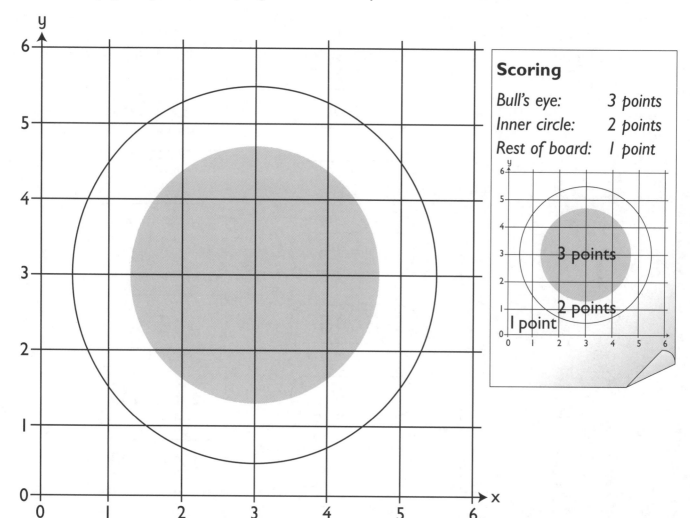

Scoring

Bull's eye: 3 points
Inner circle: 2 points
Rest of board: 1 point

Name _____ Date _____

Family holiday

● Solve word problems involving one or more steps

prices

Adult: £8.30

Child: £4.50

Adult: £452

Child: £317

Cost per day:
£95

Cost per day:
Adult: £8.30
Child: £4.50
Cost per week:
Family: £150

Use the information given above to plan a holiday to a tropical island for your own family.

Write your own word problems and work out the costs involved for your family holiday.

Name _____ Date _____

Measuring money

● **Record estimates and readings of lengths to a suitable degree of accuracy**

You can measure the diameter of a coin to the nearest millimetre like this.

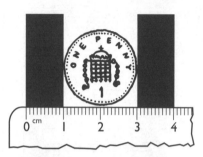
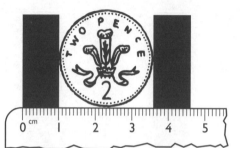

You need:
● ruler
● selection of coins

1   Measure the diameter of these coins to the nearest millimetre.

Record your measurements in three ways each time.

value of coin	☐ mm	☐ cm ☐ mm	☐ . ☐ cm
1p			
2p			
5p			
10p			
£1			

2   A school is raising money by collecting 1 kilometre of 1p coins.

The coins are placed to form straight lines. How much money do they raise with:

a 1 metre of 1p coins? ☐   **b** 10 metres of 1p coins? ☐

c 100 metres of 1p coins? ☐   **d** 1 kilometre of 1p coins? ☐

Collins
New
Primary
Maths

Name _____ Date _____

Digital digits

● **Read the time on a 24-hour digital clock and use 24-hour clock notation**

You can only use the digits **0**, **1**, **2** and **3**.

1 Write in order, the times when the DVD player will display these digits.

2 Write the matching times for the alarm clock. Colour black the correct a.m. or p.m.

DVD player display 24-hour clock				alarm display 12-hour clock				a.m. p.m.
0	1	2	3	0	1	2	3	● ○
0	1	3	2	0	1	3	2	● ○
								○ ○
								○ ○
								○ ○
								○ ○
								○ ○
								○ ○
								○ ○
								○ ○
								○ ○
								○ ○
								○ ○
								○ ○
								○ ○
								○ ○
								○ ○
								○ ○
								○ ○
								○ ○
								○ ○

3 Can the clock display 30:12? [   ] Explain: [   ]

Collins
New
Primary
Maths

Name _____ Date _____

New York cops and robbers

- **Read and plot co-ordinates**

The streets of downtown New York are built on a grid system.

1   The NYPD (New York Police Department) set up seven road blocks at these street intersections: (3, 4), (4, 3), (4, 5), (5, 2), (5, 6), (6, 5) and (7, 4).

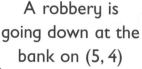

Attention all units!

A robbery is going down at the bank on (5, 4)

Plot the road blocks on the grid below.

2   The robbers escape (without any money) and make it back to their hideout by the shortest route from Bank to Hideout, avoiding all NYPD road blocks.

a   Draw their route.

b   Write the co-ordinates of each point on the escape route.

3   Write the co-ordinates of the point at which the NYPD should have placed an 8th patrol car to prevent their escape.

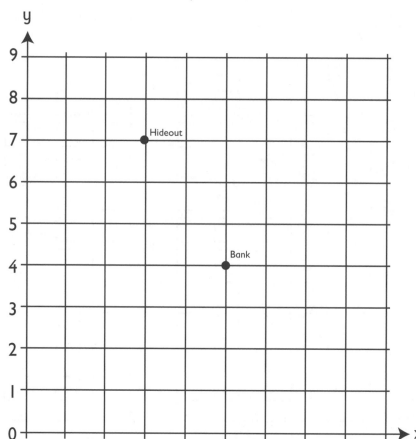

Collins New Primary Maths

Name _____ Date _____

Flower fractions

- **Use diagrams to identify equivalent fractions**

1 Colour a half of the petals on each flower.
Write the fraction you have coloured.

You need:
- coloured pencils

a 4 petals

$\dfrac{2}{4}$

b 12 petals

$\dfrac{\ }{12}$

c 8 petals

$\dfrac{\ }{8}$

d 16 petals

$\dfrac{\ }{16}$

2 Colour a third of the petals on each flower.
Write the fraction you have coloured.

a 3 petals

$\dfrac{\ }{3}$

b 9 petals

c 12 petals

d 6 petals

3 Colour a quarter of the petals on each flower. Write the fraction you have coloured.

a 4 petals

$\dfrac{\ }{4}$

b 20 petals

c 12 petals

d 8 petals

Name _____ Date _____

Water jugs

● **Solve one-step and two-step problems involving fractions and decimals**

You need:

● red, green, blue pencils

1 Look at the jug of water.

   a Shade half in green.
How many millilitres is this? ☐

   b Shade one quarter in blue.
How many millilitres is this? ☐

   c How many millilitres are
shaded altogether? ☐

   d How many millilitres are
not shaded? ☐

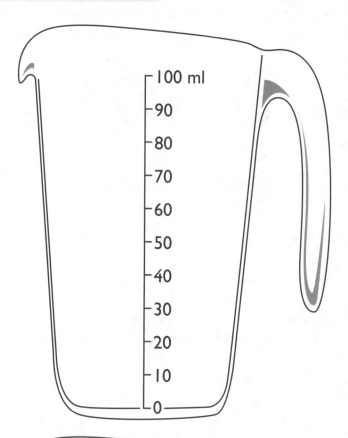

2 Look at the jug of water.

   a Shade half in green.
How many millilitres is this? ☐

   b Shade one tenth in blue.
How many millilitres is this? ☐

   c Shade two tenths in red.
How many millilitres is this? ☐

   d How many millilitres are
shaded altogether? ☐

   e How many millilitres are
not shaded? ☐

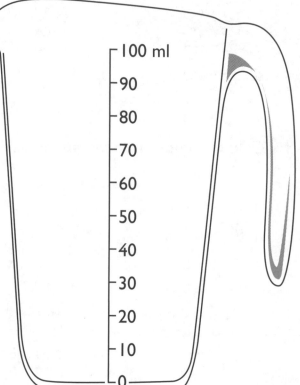

Collins
New
Primary
Maths

Name _____ Date _____

Factor trees

> ● **Find all the pairs of factors of any number up to 100**

1 Fill in the missing numbers on each factor tree.

a

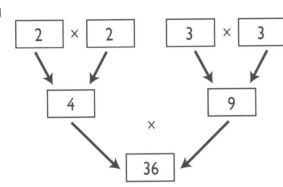

b

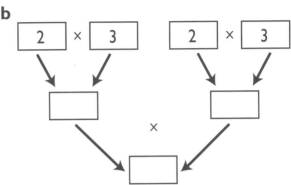

c

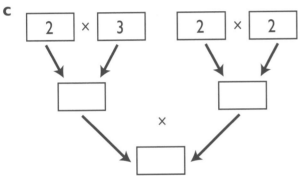

d

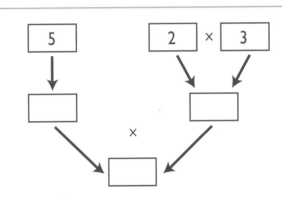

2 Fill in the missing numbers on each factor tree.

a

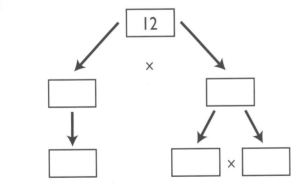

b

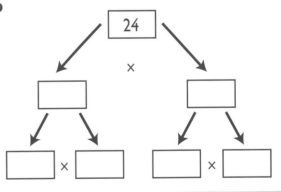

c

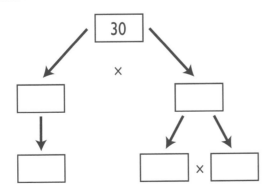

d

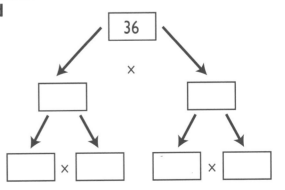

Name _____ Date _____

Multiplication methods (1)

● **Multiply a three-digit number by a one-digit number**

1 Write the multiples of 100 that each number is between.
Circle which multiple of 100 the number is closest to.

a (300) ← 327 → 400   b ☐ ← 273 → ☐   c ☐ ← 546 → ☐

d ☐ ← 193 → ☐   e ☐ ← 638 → ☐   f ☐ ← 287 → ☐

g ☐ ← 561 → ☐   h ☐ ← 725 → ☐   i ☐ ← 411 → ☐

j ☐ ← 155 → ☐   k ☐ ← 334 → ☐   l ☐ ← 455 → ☐

2 For each calculation, approximate the answer first, then use the standard method to record your work. Remember to write the numbers in the correct columns.

a 236 × 4

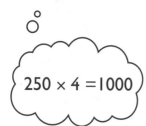

$250 \times 4 = 1000$

	2	3	6
×			4
(200 × 4)	8	0	0
(30 × 4)	1	2	0
(6 × 4)		2	4
	9	4	4

b 163 × 3

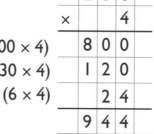

	1	6	3
×			3

c 295 × 5

	2	9	5
×			5

d 342 × 4

	3	4	2
×			4

e 278 × 5

	2	7	8
×			5

f 477 × 4

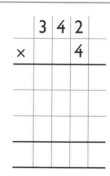

	4	7	7
×			4

48

Name _____ Date _____

Multiplication methods (2)

- ● **Multiply a pair of two-digit numbers**

For each calculation, approximate the answer first then use the grid to work out the answer.

a

25 × 34

25 × 30 = 750

×	20	5		
30	600	150		750
4	80	20	+	100
				850

b

34 × 14

×

+

_____

_____

c

27 × 35

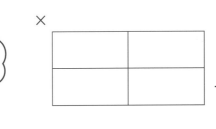

×

+

_____

_____

d

38 × 19

×

+

_____

_____

e

26 × 24

×

+

_____

_____

f

43 × 23

×

+

_____

_____

Collins
New
Primary
Maths

Name _____ Date _____

Money calculations

● **Develop calculator skills and use a calculator effectively**

Use your calculator to work out these. Give your answers in pounds and pence.

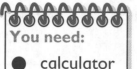

You need:
● calculator

1 a 29p + 74p =

b 241p + 159p =

c 60p + 324p =

d 58p + 231p + 79p =

2 a 93p – 46p =

b 200p – 31p =

c 924p – 638p =

d 1000p – 614p =

3 a 4 × 26p =

b 10 × 41p =

c 7 × 215p =

d 25 × 97p =

4 a 96p ÷ 6 =

b 475p ÷ 5 =

c 624p ÷ 12 =

d 1080p ÷ 8 =

5 a £1.59 + £2.38 =

b £5.32 + £6.91 =

c £4.30 + £2.50 =

d £2.27 + £1.73 =

6 a £4.79 – £2.64 =

b £2.11 – £1.73 =

c £10 – £3.65 =

d £7.50 – £4.60 =

7 a 3 × £1.85 =

b 2 × £1.73 =

c 4 × £0.63 =

d 6 × £10.40 =

8 a £6.64 ÷ 4 =

b £3.30 ÷ 5 =

c £20 ÷ 8 =

d £1.08 ÷ 12 =

Collins
New
Primary
Maths

Name _____ Date _____

Decimal investigation

● **Relate fractions to their decimal representations**

> I can find any decimal that is equivalent to a fraction using my calculator.

You need:
● calculator

1   Can you work out what Emily does?

2   What fractions can you find decimal equivalents for?

Show <u>all</u> your working out here

Collins
New
Primary
Maths

Name _____ Date _____

Percentages

● **Find percentages of numbers and quantities**

What per cent of each grid has been shaded?

What per cent has not been shaded?

Write each answer as a per cent and as a fraction.

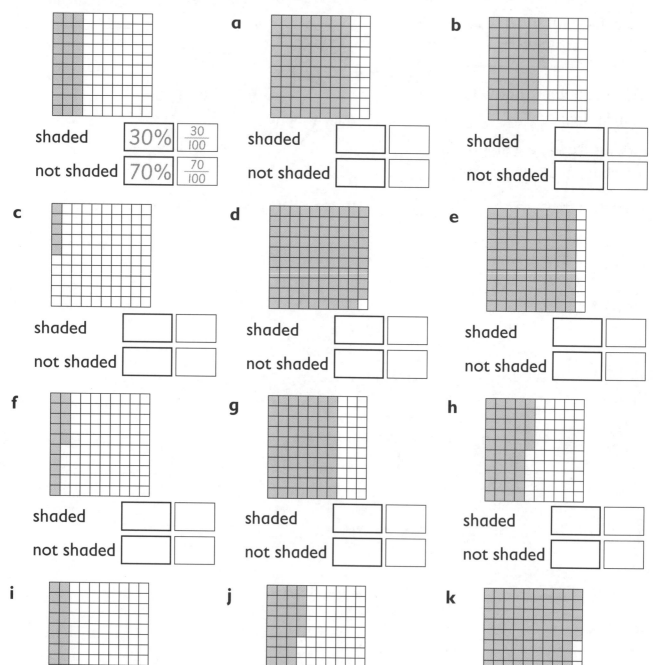

shaded $\boxed{30\%}$ $\frac{30}{100}$

not shaded $\boxed{70\%}$ $\frac{70}{100}$

a

shaded

not shaded

b

shaded

not shaded

c

shaded

not shaded

d

shaded

not shaded

e

shaded

not shaded

f

shaded

not shaded

g

shaded

not shaded

h

shaded

not shaded

i

shaded

not shaded

j

shaded

not shaded

k

shaded

not shaded

Collins
New
Primary
Maths

Name _____ Date _____

Using factors to multiply and divide

● **Use factors to multiply and divide**

1 Use factors to help you find the answers to these calculations.

Look at the worked example.

┌─────── **Example** ───────┐
│ $16 \times 5 \quad = 4 \times 4 \times 5$ │
│ $\qquad = 4 \times 20$ │
│ $\qquad = 80$ │
└────────────────────────┘

a $12 \times 5 \quad =$

$=$

$=$

b $4 \times 15 \quad =$

$=$

$=$

c $16 \times 8 \quad =$

$=$

$=$

d $24 \times 16 \quad =$

$=$

$=$

e $32 \times 12 \quad =$

$=$

$=$

f $15 \times 32 \quad =$

$=$

$=$

2 Use factors to help you find the answers to these calculations.

Look at the worked example.

┌─────── **Example** ───────┐
│ $96 \div 6 \quad = 96 \div 2 \div 3$ │
│ $\qquad = 48 \div 3$ │
│ $\qquad = 16$ │
└────────────────────────┘

a $180 \div 12 \quad =$

$=$

$=$

b $240 \div 16 \quad =$

$=$

$=$

c $360 \div 24 \quad =$

$=$

$=$

d $160 \div 32 \quad =$

$=$

$=$

e $248 \div 8 \quad =$

$=$

$=$

f $180 \div 15 \quad =$

$=$

$=$

Collins
New
Primary
Maths

Name _____ Date _____

Multiplication methods (1)

● **Multiply a three-digit number by a one-digit number**

For each calculation, approximate your answer first and write your approximation in the ring. Then work out the answer using an efficient written method of multiplication.

Check your answer using the short, standard method.

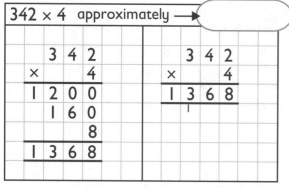

342 × 4 approximately ⟶ ◯

```
      3 4 2          3 4 2
  ×       4      ×       4
  1 2 0 0          1 3 6 8
    1 6 0
        8
  1 3 6 8
```

a | 428 × 6 approximately ⟶ ◯

```
      4 2 8          4 2 8
  ×       6      ×       6
```

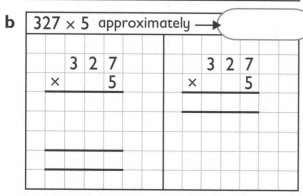

b | 327 × 5 approximately ⟶ ◯

```
      3 2 7          3 2 7
  ×       5      ×       5
```

c | 246 × 4 approximately ⟶ ◯

```
      2 4 6          2 4 6
  ×       4      ×       4
```

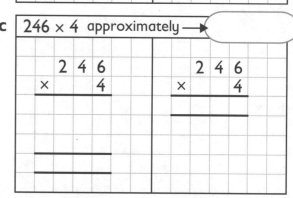

d | 473 × 6 approximately ⟶ ◯

```
      4 7 3          4 7 3
  ×       6      ×       6
```

e | 384 × 8 approximately ⟶ ◯

```
      3 8 4          3 8 4
  ×       8      ×       8
```

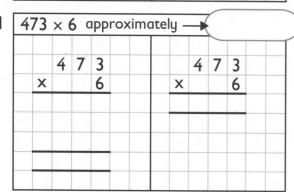

f | 568 × 7 approximately ⟶ ◯

```
      5 6 8          5 6 8
  ×       7      ×       7
```

g | 758 × 3 approximately ⟶ ◯

```
      7 5 8          7 5 8
  ×       3      ×       3
```

Collins
New
Primary
Maths

Name _____ Date _____

Multiplication methods (2)

● **Multiply a pair of two-digit numbers**

For each question, use the grid method and the clues given to work out the missing digit.

e.g. 2 | 5 | × 46

×	20	5
40	800	200
6	120	30

```
  1 0 0 0
+   1 5 0
  1 1 5 0
```

a 19 × 3 | |

×	10	9
30		
		45

```
+
  6 6 5
```

b 3 | | × 18

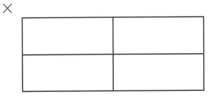

×		

```
    3 3 0
+
    5 9 4
```

c 3 | | × 42

×		

```
+     7 2
  1 5 1 2
```

d 27 × | | 6

×		

```
    1 3 5 0
+
    1 5 1 2
```

e | | 6 × 58

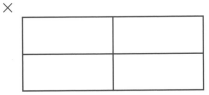

×		
3 2 0		

```
+
  2 6 6 8
```

f 24 × 6 | |

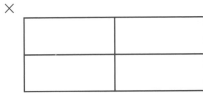

×		

```
+   1 9 2
  1 6 3 2
```

g | | | × 37

×		

```
  1 3 2 0
+   3 0 8
  1 6 2 8
```

h 39 × | | |

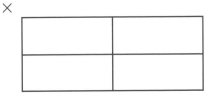

×		

```
  1 9 5 0
+   1 9 5
  2 1 4 5
```

Collins
New
Primary
Maths

Name _____ Date _____

Write your own word problems

● **Choose and use appropriate number operations to solve word problems**

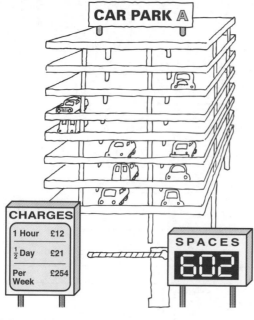

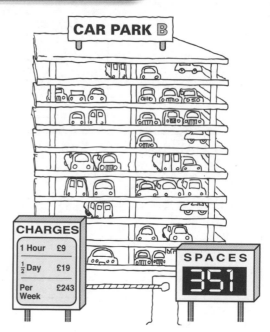

1 Use the picture above to help you write your own word problems.

2 Calculate the answers to your problems in your exercise book.

3 Give your word problems to a friend to work out.

Collins
New
Primary
Maths

Name _____Date _____

Vertical addition

● **Use efficient methods to add whole numbers**

Add these three-digit numbers.

The calculations have been written out vertically for you.

Estimate the answer to each question first and write it in the cloud.

a 263 + 252 ⟨ 520 ⟩

```
  2 6 3
+ 2 5 2
-------
  5 1 5
```

b 177 + 219

```
  1 7 7
+ 2 1 9
```

c 296 + 352

```
  2 9 6
+ 3 5 2
```

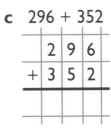

d 342 + 724

```
  3 4 2
+ 7 2 4
```

e 291 + 234

```
  2 9 1
+ 2 3 4
```

f 306 + 327

```
  3 0 6
+ 3 2 7
```

g 418 + 254

```
  4 1 8
+ 2 5 4
```

h 526 + 610

```
  5 2 6
+ 6 1 0
```

i 583 + 262

```
  5 8 3
+ 2 6 2
```

j 672 + 415

```
  6 7 2
+ 4 1 5
```

k 635 + 127

```
  6 3 5
+ 1 2 7
```

l 746 + 236

```
  7 4 6
+ 2 3 6
```

m 652 + 295

```
  6 5 2
+ 2 9 5
```

n 812 + 356

```
  8 1 2
+ 3 5 6
```

o 836 + 128

```
  8 3 6
+ 1 2 8
```

Name _____ Date _____

Money problems

- **Solve one-step problems involving money**

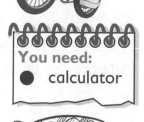

1 Work out the answers to these problems. Show all your working.

You need:
- calculator

a I have £2.68 in my purse. I spend 74p. How much do I have left?

b I earned £6.45 for my paper round. Mum gives me all the change in her purse and this adds up to 93p. How much do I have altogether?

c The pen I want costs £1.38 and the pencil case £2.15. How much money do I need?

d I have £4.95 saved. I spend £1.37. How much do I have left?

e I have £5.82. My friend has £1.09 more than me. How much does she have?

f If I save £3.70 each week for three weeks how much will I have?

2 Now check your answers on a calculator.

Collins
New
Primary
Maths

Name _____ Date _____

The multiplying and dividing machine

● Multiply and divide by 10, 100 and 1000 and understand the effect

You need:

● 40 counters (20 of one colour, 20 of another)

● paper clip   ● pencil

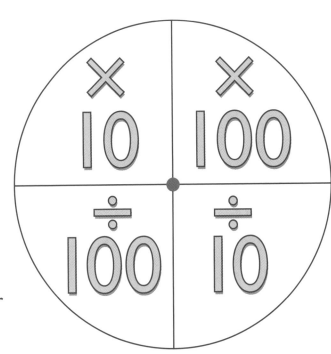

A game for 2 players.

● Take turns to choose a number from the machine, spin the spinner and perform the calculation.

● If the answer appears on the grid, cover it with one of your counters. If the number is already covered, miss a turn.

● The winner is the first player to complete a row, column or diagonal of 4 numbers.

| 7516 | 320 | 23 | 5 | | 2300 |
| 500 | 116 | 1530 | 30 | 8000 | |

230	3·2	50	751 600	3	0·23
1160	230 000	3000	153 000	32 000	15·3
751·6	153	75·16	2300	23	0·05
15 300	2·3	11·6	800 000	11 600	32
50 000	80 000	0·3	75 160	23 000	5000
300	3200	80	1·16	0·5	800

Name _____ Date _____

Multiplying by 2, 10 and 20

● **Extend mental methods for whole-number calculations**

1 Multiply each of the numbers below by 2.

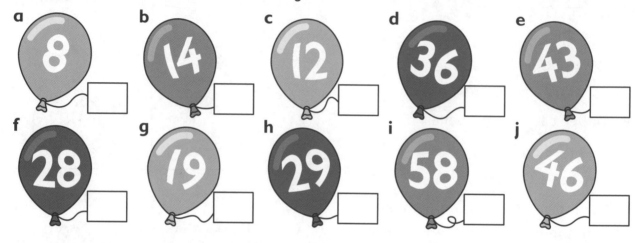

a 8 b 14 c 12 d 36 e 43

f 28 g 19 h 29 i 58 j 46

2 Multiply each of the numbers below by 10.

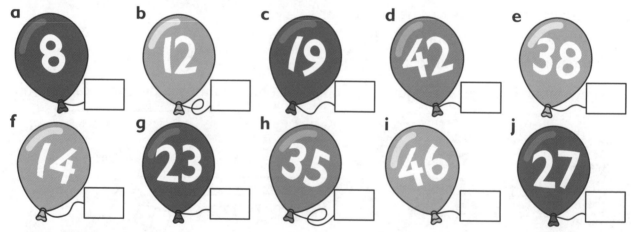

a 8 b 12 c 19 d 42 e 38

f 14 g 23 h 35 i 46 j 27

3 Multiply each of the numbers below by 20.

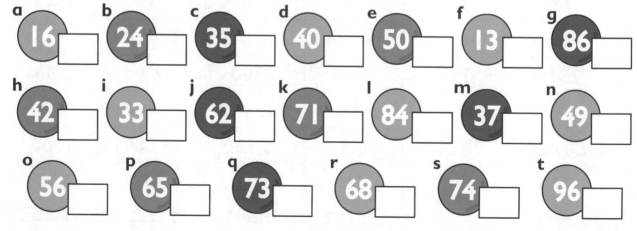

a 16 b 24 c 35 d 40 e 50 f 13 g 86

h 42 i 33 j 62 k 71 l 84 m 37 n 49

o 56 p 65 q 73 r 68 s 74 t 96

Collins New Primary Maths

Name _____ Date _____

How many hundredths?

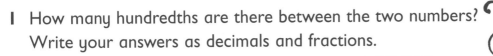

● Explain what each digit represents in whole numbers and decimals with up to two places

1 How many hundredths are there between the two numbers? Write your answers as decimals and fractions.

a 7·82 ⟶ 7·86 | 0· 04 |
                    | 4/100 |

b 8·63 ⟶ 8·67 | 0· |
                    | /100 |

c 5·12 ⟶ 5·19 | 0· |
                    | /100 |

d 6·01 ⟶ 6·10 | 0· |
                    | /100 |

e 12·56 ⟶ 12·62 | 0· |
                    | /100 |

f 15·96 ⟶ 16·03 | 0· |
                    | /100 |

g 24·89 ⟶ 24·99 | 0· |
                    | /100 |

h 27·35 ⟶ 27·49 | 0· |
                    | /100 |

2 Write pairs of decimal numbers with up to two places that have the following differences.

a [   ] 0·14 [   ]

b [   ] 0·07 [   ]

c [   ] 0·25 [   ]

d [   ] 0·31 [   ]

e [   ] 0·43 [   ]

Name _____ Date _____

Money problems

- Use a calculator to solve problems

Work out the answers to these questions using the standard method or a mental method. Then check your answers on the calculator.

a My bill came to £3.01. I bought a packet of nuts and two cereal bars. What is the price of one cereal bar?

b How much would it cost to buy one pack of everything except the cereal bar?

c Three friends bought two bags of oranges each. How much do they need to pay altogether?

d If I buy two packs of strawberries and two bags of oranges, how much will I spend?

e Every day for my lunch I buy a pack of sandwiches and a packet of nuts. How much will I spend in a five-day week?

Bigger and smaller

● **Multiply and divide by 10, 100 and 1000 and understand the effect**

You need:

● 40 counters (20 of one colour, 20 of another)

● paper clip   ● pencil

A game for 2 players.

● Take turns to choose a number from the machine, spin the spinner and perform the calculation.

● If the answer appears on the grid, cover it with one of your counters. If the number is already covered, miss a turn.

● The winner is the first player to complete a row, column or diagonal of 4 numbers.

| 62 | 751 | 400 | 2500 | 800 | 12·8 |
| 5 | 950 | 8420 | 3124 | 3·7 | 175·1 |

80	75·1	37	12 800	25	40 000
3 124 000	7510	500	84·2	0·8	1·28
0·62	250 000	2·5	400 000	4	9·5
31 240	17·51	0·37	8·42	62 000	1751
0·4	6·2	17 510	80 000	8 420 000	95
950 000	7·51	31.24	3700	0·05	312.4

Collins New Primary Maths

Name _____ Date _____

Multiplying by 12, 19 and 21

Remember
1 dozen = 12

● **Extend mental methods for whole-number calculations**

1 Work out the answers to these word problems.

a Eggs are packed in boxes of 12. How many eggs are in 14 boxes?

b The florist sold 23 dozen red roses. How many roses are there altogether?

c For the school picnic, cook ordered 36 dozen bread rolls. How many rolls is this?

d The supermarket had family packs of crisps on sale. Mum bought six packs. There were 19 small packets inside. How many small packets of crisps were there altogether?

e Orange juice is packed in cartons of 21. The junior teachers bought 28 cartons. How many children could have orange juice in the junior school?

f The corner shop had 32 dozen eggs on the shelf. Half of them were broken. How many eggs could be sold?

The 12, 19 or 21 game

A game for 2 players.

● Start the timer.

● Multiply the number cards by 12, 19 or 21 to find the matching answer.

● Write the number from the number card above the correct number on the grid.

● The first player to complete the grid is the winner.

How long did you take to complete the game?

You need:

● stopwatch or clock

264	323	924	693
1140	612	168	231
855	348	1235	798

Collins New Primary Maths

Name _____ Date _____

Add and take away

● Use knowledge of place value and addition and
subtraction to derive sums and differences

1 Add these numbers together.

a 5 + 6 = ☐   **b** 7 + 3 = ☐   **c** 2 + 9 = ☐

d 8 + 5 = ☐   **e** 4 + 7 = ☐   **f** 5 + 7 = ☐

g 30 + 40 = ☐   **h** 50 + 60 = ☐   **i** 80 + 30 = ☐

j 10 + 70 = ☐   **k** 60 + 30 = ☐   **l** 70 + 50 = ☐

2 Practise your addition of two-digit numbers, add the tens first and then the units.

a 24 + 45 = ☐   **b** 47 + 52 = ☐   **c** 36 + 54 = ☐

   20 + 40 = ☐   40 + 50 = ☐   30 + 50 = ☐

   4 + 5 = ☐   7 + 2 = ☐   6 + 4 = ☐

d 48 + 51 = ☐   **e** 68 + 45 = ☐   **f** 42 + 58 = ☐

   40 + 50 = ☐   60 + 40 = ☐   40 + 50 = ☐

   8 + 1 = ☐   8 + 5 = ☐   2 + 8 = ☐

3 Practise subtracting two-digit numbers, take away the tens first and then the units.

a 84 − 36 = ☐   **b** 73 − 42 = ☐   **c** 68 − 27 = ☐

   84 − 30 = 54   73 − 40 = ☐   68 − 20 = ☐

   54 − 6 = ☐   ☐ − 2 = ☐   ☐ − 7 = ☐

d 75 − 37 = ☐   **e** 66 − 48 = ☐   **f** 76 − 43 = ☐

   75 − 30 = ☐   66 − 40 = ☐   76 − 40 = ☐

   ☐ − 7 = ☐   ☐ − 8 = ☐   ☐ − 3 = ☐

Name _____ Date _____

Simple statements

● **Explore properties and propose a general statement about numbers**

1 Look at each statement, work out the calculations and find out if the statement is true or false. Write another calculation in the (cloud) to justify your decision.

a An even number add an even number is always an even number.

6 + 8 = ☐   12 + 14 = ☐

20 + 16 = ☐   18 + 24 = ☐

120 + 44 = ☐

Is the statement true or false? ☐

b An odd number add an odd number is always even.

5 + 7 = ☐   11 + 15 = ☐

17 + 13 = ☐   25 + 29 = ☐

99 + 31 = ☐

Is the statement true or false? ☐

c An odd number add an even number is always even.

3 + 8 = ☐   7 + 28 = ☐

35 + 46 = ☐   67 + 38 = ☐

113 + 64 = ☐

Is the statement true or false? ☐

2 Three even numbers added together always make an odd number. This time make up your own calculations to test the statement.

Is the statement true or false? ☐

C. Collins
New
Primary
Maths

Name _____ Date _____

Doubling and halving whole numbers

- **Double and halve 2-digit numbers**

1 Double each number.

Example

18 × 2 = 36

a 18	**b** 86	**c** 46	**d** 75
e 54	**f** 84	**g** 37	**h** 95
i 29	**j** 39	**k** 63	**l** 92

2 Halve each number.

Example

92 ÷ 2 = 46

a 92	**b** 30	**c** 66	**d** 28
e 54	**f** 72	**g** 46	**h** 74
i 90	**j** 82	**k** 8	**l** 34

LOSE HALF YOUR WEIGHT!

Name _____ Date _____

Count in steps of 25 game

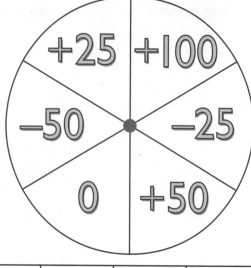

● **Recognise and extend number sequences**

A game for 2 players.

● Both players place their counter on 0. Take turns to spin the spinner.

● Move your counter forwards or backwards 25 or 50 as shown on the spinner. If you spin 0 you miss a go.

● The winner is the first person to reach 1000 exactly.

You need:
● paper clip
● pencil
● 2 counters

−1000	−975	−950	−925	−900	−875	−850	−825	−800
−775	−750	−725	−700	−675	−650	−625	−600	−575
−550	−525	−500	−475	−450	−425	−400	−375	−350
−325	−300	−275	−250	−225	−200	−175	−150	−125
−100	−75	−50	−25	0	25	50	75	100
125	150	175	200	225	250	275	300	325
350	375	400	425	450	475	500	525	550
575	600	625	650	675	700	725	750	775
800	825	850	875	900	925	950	975	1000

Collins
New
Primary
Maths

Name _____ Date _____

Getting in shape

● **Say whether a triangle is isosceles, equilateral or scalene**

1   Draw a straight line with your
    ruler to complete each triangle.

You need:
● ruler

Triangle names

equilateral: all three sides equal
isosceles: two sides equal
scalene: no two sides equal

2   Measure the sides
    of each triangle.
    Write its name in the box.

a
3 cm
3 cm
3 cm

b

c

d

e

f

g

h

i

Name _____ Date _____

Missing mirror lines

- **Recognise where a shape will be after reflection in a mirror line**

These shapes have been reflected but the mirror lines are missing.

Use your mirror to find the position of each mirror line.

Carefully rule dotted lines to represent each mirror line.

You need:
- mirror
- ruler

mirror line

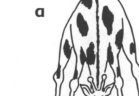

a

b

c

d

e

f

g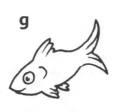

 **h**

Collins
New
Primary
Maths

Name _____ Date _____

Filling gaps

● Use knowledge of place value and addition and subtraction to derive sums and differences

Fill in the gaps.

a   400 + ☐ + 200 + 100 = 1300

b   726 + ☐ = 1526

c   900 + 300 + 600 + ☐ = 2300

d   874 + ☐ =1474

e   ☐ + 800 + 200 + 500 = 2000

f   ☐ − 500 = 846

g   580 + ☐ = 870

h   ☐ − 700 = 518

i   ☐ + 520 = 1190

j   1462 − ☐ = 562

k   820 + ☐ = 1180

l   472 + ☐ = 852

m   930 − ☐ = 480

n   ☐ + 420 = 932

o   ☐ − 570 = 240

p   667 + ☐ = 1017

q   680 − ☐ =390

r   ☐ − 420 = 152

s   ☐ + 500 = 1185

t   ☐ − 270 = 587

Collins New Primary Maths

Name _____ Date _____

Problems of your own

● **Represent a problem by identifying and recording the calculations**

● For each calculation below, secretly substitute the diamond (◇) for an operation: +, −, × or ÷
Then write a word problem using that calculation.

● When you have written your five word problems, swap sheets with a friend and work out the answers to their five word problems.

$56 + 48$

● Then swap back and check answers.

---

56 ◇ 48

---

436 ◇ 201

---

75 ◇ 6 ◇ 42

---

133 ◇ 8

---

96 ◇ 52 ◇ 67

Collins New Primary Maths

Name _____ Date _____

Doubling and halving whole numbers

● **Double and halve whole numbers**

1 Find the multiples of 100. Double them. Record your answer as a multiplication number sentence.

You need:
● calculator

9500   3700   7600   9623

4100   8400   2510   5800

6200   10 000   5619

3745   2300   7002

2 Find the multiples of 100. Halve them. Record your answer as a division number sentence.

16 200   13 415   11 000   20 000

14 600   13 400   19 004   17 800

15 400   15 310   17 627

18 600   19 800   12 200

3 Halve each of these numbers.
Show all your working on the back of this sheet.
Check your answer is correct by performing the inverse operation on your calculator.

a 8700	**b** 11 200	**c** 14 900
d 20 600	**e** 16 300	**f** 10 400
g 9700	**h** 13 500	**i** 18 900
j 15 800	**k** 12 500	**l** 17 400

Name _____ Date _____

Finding out about multiples of 3 and 6

● **Make and investigate a general statement about familiar numbers**

Investigation 1

● Look at the 1-100 number square.

● Continue to cross out the multiples of 3 from 3 to 99.

● For each multiple of 3, add together the digits that make up the number, e.g. 18 = 1 + 8 = 9

● If the answer is another two-digit number, add these two digits together until you get a one-digit number,
e.g. 39 = 3 + 9 = 12
       12 = 1 + 2 = 2

● What do you notice?

1	2	X	4	5	X	7	8	9	10
11	12	13	14	15	16	17	18	19	20
21	22	23	24	25	26	27	28	29	30
31	32	33	34	35	36	37	38	39	40
41	42	43	44	45	46	47	48	49	50
51	52	53	54	55	56	57	58	59	60
61	62	63	64	65	66	67	68	69	70
71	72	73	74	75	76	77	78	79	80
81	82	83	84	85	86	87	88	89	90
91	92	93	94	95	96	97	98	99	100

Investigation 2

● Repeat the steps for Investigation 1 using this 101-201 number square

● What do you notice?

Write a statement showing what you found out about the multiples of 3.

101	102	103	104	105	106	107	108	109	110
111	112	113	114	115	116	117	118	19	120
121	122	123	124	125	126	127	128	129	130
131	132	133	134	135	136	137	138	139	140
141	142	143	144	145	146	147	148	149	150
151	152	153	154	155	156	157	158	159	160
161	162	163	164	165	166	167	168	169	170
171	172	173	174	175	176	177	178	179	180
181	182	183	184	185	186	187	188	189	190
191	192	193	194	195	196	197	198	199	200

Taking it further

● Using the two number squares above, repeat investigations 1 and 2, this time drawing a circle around the multiples of 6 from 6 to 198.

1	2	X	4	5	⊗	7	8	9	10
11	12	13	14	15	16	17	18	19	20

101	102	103	104	105	106	107	108	109	110
111	112	113	114	115	116	117	118	19	120

● Write a statement showing what you found out about the multiples of 6.

Name _____ Date _____

Mountain building

● **Solve mathematical problems or puzzles**

1   Complete these sentences.

The 1st mountain is built with 4 pegs.

The 2nd mountain is built with ☐ pegs.

The 3rd mountain is built with ☐ pegs.

2   Draw the 4th mountain.

The 4th mountain is built with ☐ pegs.

3   Complete the first part of this table with
your results.

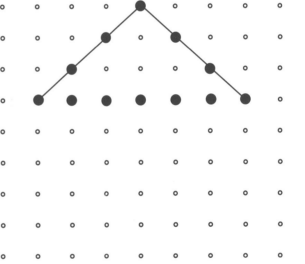

mountain	number of pegs
1st	4
2nd	
3rd	
4th	
7th	
10th	

4   Look at the first four entries in your
table. Write about the pattern you notice.

5   Use your pattern to work out the number of pegs needed to build the
7th and 10th mountains. Write these in the table.

6   Write down a rule for finding the
number of pegs needed to build a
mountain of any size.

7   The 100th mountain will need 400 pegs to build.

True or false? ☐   Why? ☐

Name _____ Date _____

Lines on a 9-dot grid

● Recognise perpendicular and parallel lines

1 In grids 1 to 30 find as many different ways to draw two parallel lines as you can. The lines must be straight, between 2 dots, without crossing a dot.

2 In each grid draw, in red, a perpendicular line which joins the two parallel lines.

Example

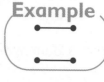

Example

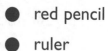

You need:
● red pencil
● ruler

1	2	3	4	5
6	7	8	9	10
11	12	13	14	15
16	17	18	19	20
21	22	23	24	25
26	27	28	29	30

Collins New Primary Maths

Name _____ Date _____

Guessing weights

● **Record estimates and readings from scales to a suitable degree of accuracy**

Guess the weight of the cake	
Name	**Guess**
Wayne	3·2 kg
Tim	3·9 kg
Georgia	3·65 kg
Emma	3·35 kg
Harry	3·8 kg
Ian	3·4 kg

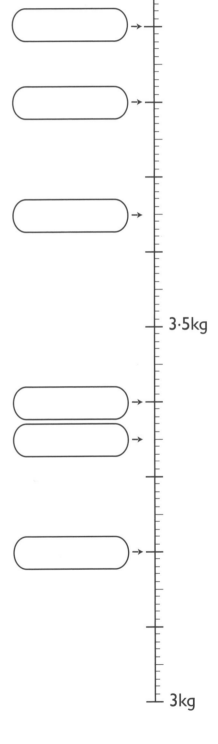

1　Write each child's name on the correct label.

2　The cake weighed 3·5 kg.

   a What was the guessed weight of the cake nearest to 3·5 kg?

   b Who won the cake?

3　Round each weight to the nearest whole kilogram.

Weight	Nearest whole kilogram
3·2 kg	3 kg
3·9 kg	
3·65 kg	
3·35 kg	
3·8 kg	
3·4 kg	

Name _____ Date _____

Tennis bar charts

● **Collect and organise data to answer a question**

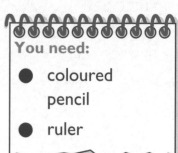

1   Count the number of games of tennis each person played.

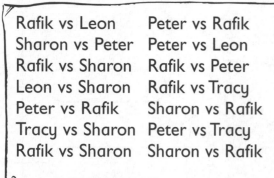

Rafik vs Leon   Peter vs Rafik   Rafik vs Peter
Sharon vs Peter   Peter vs Leon   Sharon vs Peter
Rafik vs Sharon   Rafik vs Peter   Peter vs Rafik
Leon vs Sharon   Rafik vs Tracy   Leon vs Rafik
Peter vs Rafik   Sharon vs Rafik   Rafik vs Leon
Tracy vs Sharon   Peter vs Tracy   Leon vs Rafik
Rafik vs Sharon   Sharon vs Rafik

You need:

● coloured
   pencil
● ruler

2   Record the totals in this table.

Player	Number of games played
Rafik	
Sharon	
Peter	
Leon	
Tracy	

3   Complete the bar chart.

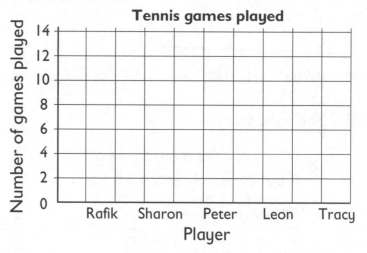

Tennis games played

(y-axis: Number of games played, 0–14; x-axis: Player — Rafik, Sharon, Peter, Leon, Tracy)

4   Use the information in the bar chart to answer these questions:

a How many times did Sharon play?

b Who played 9 times?

c Who played the most?

d How many times did Tracy or Peter play?

e How many more times did Peter play than Leon?

f Who played less than Sharon?

g Who played more than 8 times?

Collins New Primary Maths

Name _____ Date _____

Batteries

● **Draw line graphs**

Batteries cost
£2 each.

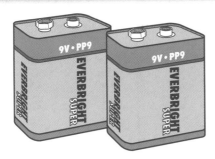

1 Copy and complete the table.

Number of batteries	Cost (£)
0	0
1	2
2	4
3	6
4	
5	
6	
7	
8	

2 Complete the bar line chart.

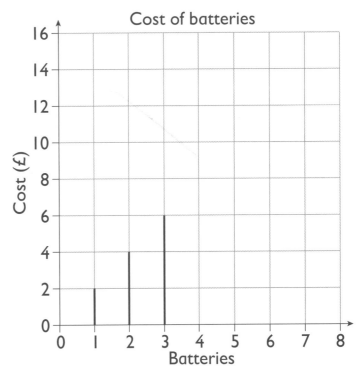

3 Mark the top of each bar line using a cross.

4 Join the crosses using straight lines to make a line graph.

5 Use the information in the line graph to answer these questions.

   a How much do 5 batteries cost?

   b How many batteries could you buy for £14?

   c Maria has £9. How many batteries can she buy?

6 Which points on the line have meaning? Which points do not have meaning?

Name _____ Date _____

Office temperature

● **Present data using a line graph**

The table shows the temperature in an office every hour.

Time	Temperature
11:00 a.m.	21
12 noon	23
1:00 p.m.	18
2:00 p.m.	22
3:00 p.m.	21
4:00 p.m.	22
5:00 p.m.	17
6:00 p.m.	15

1 Complete the bar line chart.

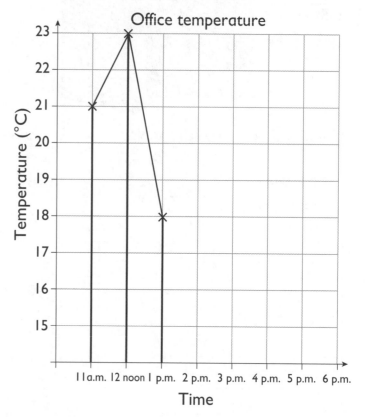

2 Mark the top of each bar line using a cross.

3 Join the crosses using straight lines to make a line graph.

4 Use the information in the line graph to answer these questions.

 a What was the highest temperature in the office?

 b When was the temperature 22 °C?

 c What happened to the temperature after 4.00 p.m.?

 d What was the difference in temperature between 11.00 a.m. and 6.00 p.m.?

5 Which points on the line graph have meaning?

Name _____ Date _____

A piece of cake

● **Solve simple problems or puzzles involving mass**

Before the restaurant chef places his cakes in the chill cabinet, he divides each cake into six approximately equal pieces.

You need:
● ruler

1 Draw straight lines to show where he will cut each cake.

2 Work out the weight of each slice.

a 4·8 kg

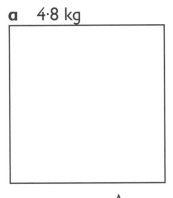

b 5·1 kg

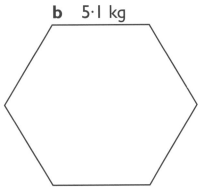

c 3·9 kg

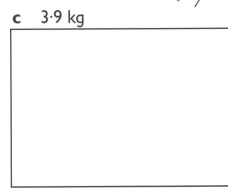

d 4·44 kg

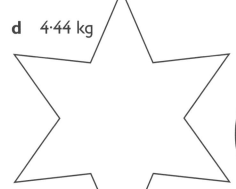

e 4·62 kg

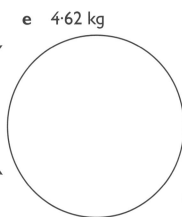

f 5·46 kg

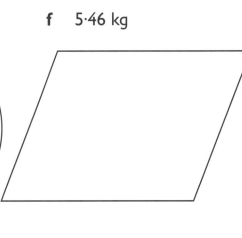

3 Tom and Joyce each have a slice of cake **b**. Work out the weight, in kilograms, of cake **b** which is left for other customers.

4 The order for table 7 is 3 slices of cake **c** and 1 slice of cake **f**. What weight of cake does the waiter carry to the table?

5 At closing time, all the cakes have been eaten except for 1 slice each of cakes **a**, **d** and **e**. What weight of leftover cake, to the nearest whole kilogram, does the chef place in the refrigerator?

Name _____ Date _____

Ace serves

● **Collect and organise data to answer a question**

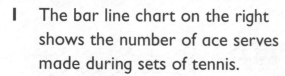

1 The bar line chart on the right shows the number of ace serves made during sets of tennis.

The number of ace serves ranged from 2 to 8.

4 aces were served in 16 sets.

a Complete the bar line chart.

b What is the mode?

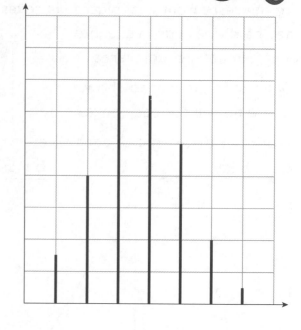

2 Make up your own data for the same bar line chart on the right.

The horizontal axis represents time. It could be days, months, years, minutes, hours, etc.

Decide what the vertical axis will represent. Choose something that changes over time.

Decide on realistic numbers for the vertical axis and work out the scale.

If you joined the tops of your bar lines, would the points in between make sense?

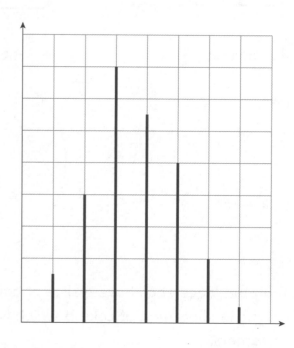

Time

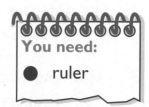

You need:
● ruler

Collins
New
Primary
Maths

Name _____ Date _____

More multiplication tables

● **Construct line graphs**

Work in pairs.

One person is to work on the 12 times table, the other person on the 13 times table.

1   Copy and complete your multiplication table.

0 × 12 = 0	0 × 13 = 0
1 × 12 = 12	1 × 13 = 13
2 × 12 = 24	2 × 13 = 26

2   Draw a line graph for your table. Make your graph as big as possible. Choose a sensible scale for the vertical axis.

3   Take turns to ask each other questions about the other person's line graph.

For example:

What is 4·5 × 12?   What is 6·4 × 13?

What is 90 ÷ 12?   What is 72 ÷ 13?

4   Check each other's answers using a calculator.

Name _____ Date _____

Sports trophy graph

● **Present data using a line graph**

The children of Chumley School saved money each week for a sports trophy.

They stuck a coloured square on their chart for each £2 saved.

They counted their money every fortnight. By the end of week 2, they had stuck 10 squares, so they had saved £20.

You need:

● graph paper

● ruler

I Count the squares to work out how much they had saved by the end of each fortnight. Now complete the table.

Week	Savings (£)
0	0
2	20
4	
6	
8	
10	

2 Look at the example and draw a line graph to show your results.

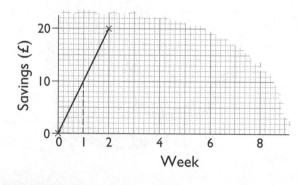

3 Use your line graph to estimate how much was saved:

a at the end of week 1

b at the end of week 3

c at the end of week 7

d at the end of week 9

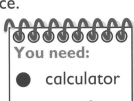

Name _____ Date _____

School problems

● **Solve one-step problems involving whole numbers**

1 Work this problem out in your head and make jottings in the space.

The school rabbits are really greedy. On Monday they ate 14 carrots, on Tuesday they ate 16 carrots, on Wednesday they ate 15 and on Thursday 13. We did not give them any on Friday! How many did they eat altogether?

You need:
● calculator

2 Work this problem out using a written method.

The school is collecting tokens for books. 318 were brought in last week and 451 this week. How many have been brought in so far?

3 Work this problem out using a calculator. Write down the calculation you do in the space.

765 parents came to the school on parents' evening. 342 were Dads. How many were Mums?

Name _____ Date _____

Reviewing multiplication

● **Use efficient written methods to multiply HTU × U, TU × TU and U.t × U**

For each calculation, approximate the answer first, then use the grid to work out the answer.

a 354 × 3 ○○

×	300	50	4	
3				=

b 612 × 8 ○○

×	600	10	2	
8				=

c 584 × 6 ○○

×				
				=

d 7·8 × 7 ○○

×	7·0	0·8	
7			=

e 3·9 × 4 ○○

×	3·0	0·9	
4			=

f 5·6 × 6 ○○

×			
			=

g 62 × 48 ○○

×	60	2	
40			
8			=

h 23 × 76 ○○

×	20	3	
70			
6			=

i 18 × 55 ○○

×			
			=

86

© Collins New Primary Maths

Name _____ Date _____

Leafy areas

● **Understand area measured in square centimetres (cm²)**

This beech leaf has an area of about 13 cm².

1   Write your estimates in the table, then count the squares on the leaves and find their approximate area.

You need:
● ruler

1	2	3	
4	5	6	7
	beech		
8	9	10	11
		12	13

lime

sycamore

ivy

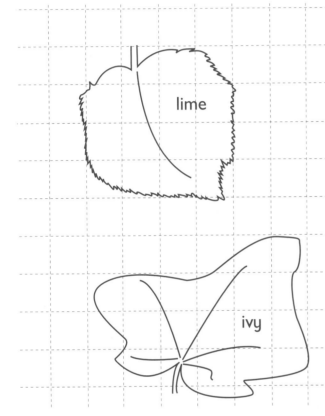
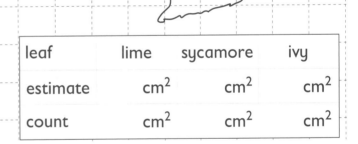

leaf	lime	sycamore	ivy
estimate	cm²	cm²	cm²
count	cm²	cm²	cm²

2   Find the area of these leaves. Draw the missing lines to help you.

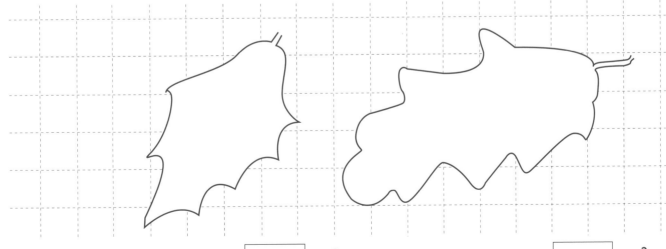

Area of holly leaf is about [   ] cm².   Area of oak leaf is about [   ] cm².

Name _____ Date _____

Reading scales in grams

● **Work out the reading between two unnumbered divisions on kitchen scales**

1 Write the weight shown by each arrow on the scales.

a [200] g

b [   ] g

c [   ] g

d [   ] g

e [   ] g

f [   ] g

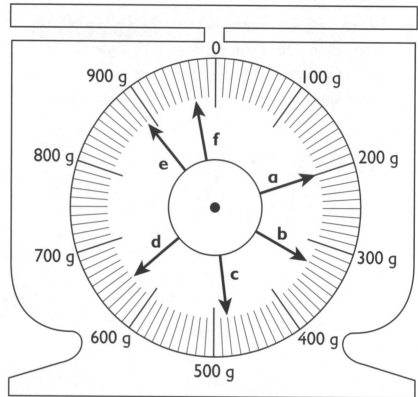

2 Draw arrows on the scales to show each of these weights. Label each arrow.

A 60 g

B 110 g

C 370 g

D 550 g

E 780 g

F 930 g

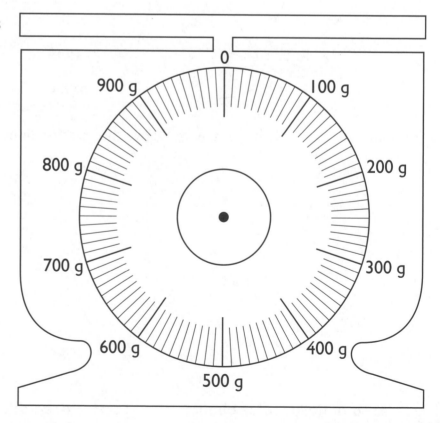

Collins
New
Primary
Maths

Name _____ Date _____

Line up the decimals

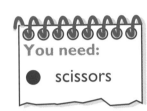

● Order a set of numbers or measurements with the same number of decimal places

You can play on your own or with a partner.

You need:
● scissors

● Cut out the cards and shuffle them. If you are playing with a friend, share out the cards.

● Place your cards in a pile face down in front of you.

● Take turns to turn over the top card from your pile and place it on the grid. The cards must all be placed in order. Once cards have been put on the grid, they can't be moved. If a card can't be placed on the grid in order, put the card near you to one side.

● When you have turned over all your cards, count how many cards aren't on the grid. This is your score.

● The player with the lower score is the winner. If you are playing on your own, play again to beat your score.

2·54	3·85	6·14
6·41	8·5	4·87
9·84	5·64	3·15
7·66	7·91	1·7
2·3	9·52	4·39

0

10

Collins
New
Primary
Maths

Name _____ Date _____

Multiplication puzzles

● Use efficient written methods to multiply HTU × U, TU × TU and U.t × U

1 Solve the multiplication puzzles using a written method.

a Multiply the sum of 18 and 14 by the sum of 23 and 58.

b Multiply the sum of 26 and 47 by the sum of 19 and 18.

c Multiply the difference between 385 and 263 by the difference between 38 and 32.

d Multiply the difference between 67 and 36 by the difference between 81 and 43.

e Multiply the sum of 26 and 55 by the difference between 76 and 35.

f Multiply the sum of 3·8 and 4·4 by the difference between 96 and 89.

2 Write a different two-digit number in each circle and then write the answer in the box. Use the back of this sheet to show all your working.

a 53 × ◯ = ☐

b 86 × ◯ = ☐

3 Write a different one-digit number in each circle and then write the answer in the box. Use the back of this sheet to show all your working.

a ◯ × 7·2 = ☐

b ◯ × 434 = ☐

Collins New Primary Maths

Name _____ Date _____

Changing shapes

● **Read and plot co-ordinates in the first quadrant**

1 Write the co-ordinates of these points.

A (2, 1)

B _____

C _____

D _____

E _____

F _____

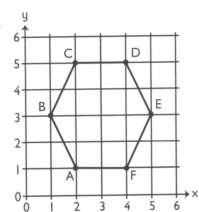

You need:
● ruler

2 Double the x-co-ordinate
of the points A to F.

A (4, 1)

B _____

C _____

D _____

E _____

F _____

Plot the points and join them to
make a new shape on the grid.

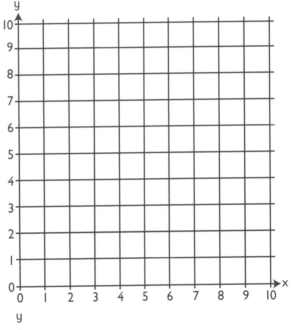

3 Double the y-co-ordinate
of the points A to F in question 1.

A (2, 2)

B _____

C _____

D _____

E _____

F _____

Plot the points and join them to
make a new shape on the grid.

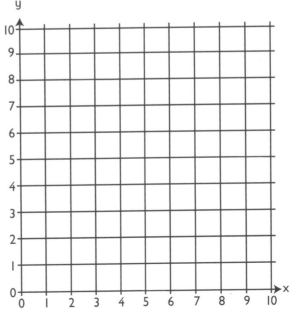

Name _____ Date _____

Framing photos

● **Use the formula 'length × breadth' for the area of a rectangle**

This photograph has an area of 4 cm². The frame and the photograph together have an area of 16 cm². The frame alone has an area of 12 cm².

1   Draw frames round each photograph.
     Complete the table.

Dimensions of photograph	Area of		
	photo and frame (cm²)	photo only (cm²)	frame only (cm²)
1 cm × 1 cm			
2 cm × 2 cm			
3 cm × 3 cm			
4 cm × 4 cm			
5 cm × 5 cm			
6 cm × 6 cm			

2   What if you had a 10 cm × 10 cm photo? What is the area of the frame? [   ] cm²

92

Name _____ Date _____

Colouring fractions

● **Explain reasoning using diagrams**

Colour in the shapes. Describe each coloured fraction as an improper fraction and as a mixed number.

Colour in 5 quarters.

Improper fraction $\dfrac{5}{4}$

Mixed number $1\dfrac{1}{4}$

a Colour in 3 halves

Improper fraction $\dfrac{}{2}$

Mixed number $\dfrac{}{2}$

b Colour in 7 sixths

Improper fraction $\dfrac{}{6}$

Mixed number $\dfrac{}{6}$

c Colour in 5 thirds

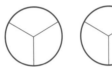

Improper fraction $\dfrac{}{3}$

Mixed number $\dfrac{}{3}$

d Colour in 8 fifths.

Improper fraction $\dfrac{}{5}$

Mixed number $\dfrac{}{5}$

e Colour in 10 sevenths.

Improper fraction $\dfrac{}{7}$

Mixed number $\dfrac{}{7}$

f Colour in 16 tenths.

Improper fraction $\dfrac{}{}$

Mixed number $\dfrac{}{}$

g Colour in 11 eighths.

Improper fraction $\dfrac{}{}$

Mixed number $\dfrac{}{}$

Name _____ Date _____

Fraction tenths and decimal tenths

● **Relate fractions to their decimal equivalents**

Label the pictures in fractions and decimals.

a

$\frac{3}{10}$ or 0·3 of the chocolate is shaded

b
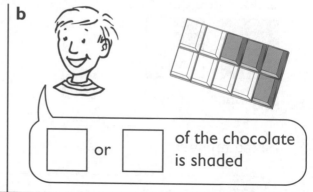

☐ or ☐ of the chocolate is shaded

c
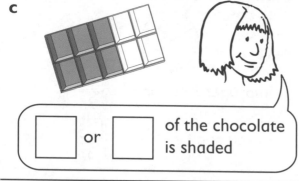

☐ or ☐ of the chocolate is shaded

d
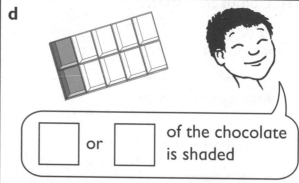

☐ or ☐ of the chocolate is shaded

e
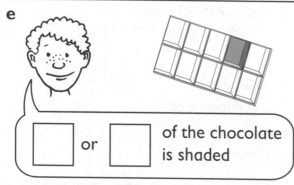

☐ or ☐ of the chocolate is shaded

f

☐ or ☐ of the chocolate is shaded

g

☐ or ☐ of the chocolate is shaded

h

☐ or ☐ of the chocolate is shaded

Collins
New
Primary
Maths

Name _____ Date _____

Percentages

● **Understand percentages as the number of parts in every 100**

1   Shade the grid in the following percentages and colours.

a 40% blue   **b** 10% red   **c** 20% green   **d** 30% yellow

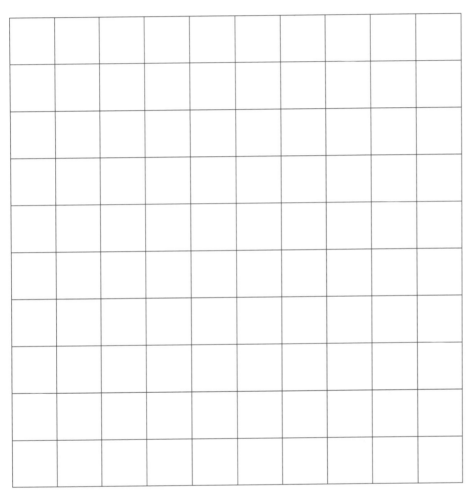

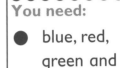

You need:

● blue, red, green and yellow coloured pencils

2   Now answer these questions.

   a What fraction of the grid is red?

   b What fraction of the grid is blue?

   c What fraction of the grid is yellow?

   d What fraction of the grid is green and yellow?

   e What fraction of the grid is not green?

Name _____ Date _____

Proportion problems

● **Solve simple problems involving proportions of quantities**

Complete the tables and work out the answers to the problems.
Use the pictures to help you.

a I am planting flower seeds. For every one pink seed, I plant 3 blue seeds.

If I plant 20 seeds, how many pink and blue flowers will I have?

pink [＿＿＿＿]   blue [＿＿＿＿]

Flowers		
Pink	**Blue**	**Total**
1	3	4
		20

b When we eat biscuits, I eat one and my brother eats 4! If I ate 6, how many would my brother have eaten?

[＿＿＿＿＿＿＿＿＿＿＿＿＿＿＿＿]

Biscuits	
Me	**My brother**
1	
2	
3	
4	
5	
6	

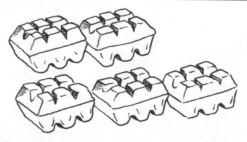

c In every box of eggs, there are 5 brown eggs and one white. I have 5 boxes of eggs. How many of each colour egg will I have?

brown [＿＿＿＿]   white [＿＿＿＿]

	Eggs	
Boxes	**Brown**	**White**
1		
2		
3		
4		
5		

Collins
New
Primary
Maths

Name _____ Date _____

Helpful doubles

- ● **Use doubling to multiply**

1 Complete each number fact for 4 by doubling and doubling again.

a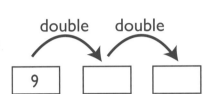

b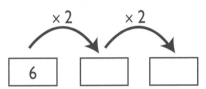

c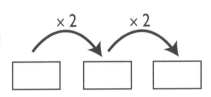

d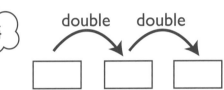

2 Complete each number fact for 8 by multiplying by 4 then doubling your answer.

a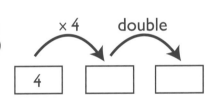

b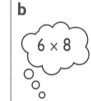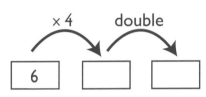

c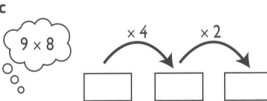

d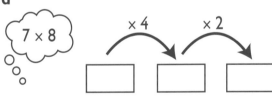

3 Complete each number fact for 16 by multiplying by 8 then doubling your answer.

a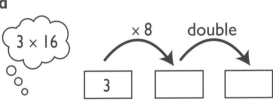

b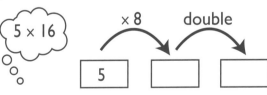

c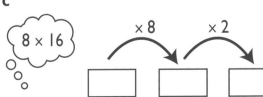

d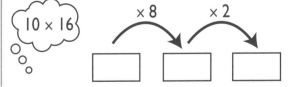

Name _____ Date _____

Exchange rates

● **Make simple conversions of pounds to foreign currency**

TOURIST RATES £1=		
AUSTRALIA	(dollars)	2
BELGIUM	(euros)	2
SAUDI ARABIA	(riyal)	6
DENMARK	(kroner)	12
INDIA	(rupees)	60
JAPAN	(yen)	150
FINLAND	(euros)	2
THAILAND	(baht)	55
U.S.A.	(dollars)	2

1   Which currency is used in

Belgium [   ]   Japan [   ]

USA [   ]   Australia [   ]

2   What is the exchange rate for

Danish kroner [   ]

Indian rupees [   ]

Japanese yen [   ]

Finnish euros? [   ]

3   The table above shows how many of each currency I receive if I change £1.
How many of these currencies do I receive if I change £2?

Danish kroner   [12 × 2 = 24 kroner]

Thai baht   [   ]

Finnish euros   [   ]

Japanese yen   [   ]

What do I recieve if I change £5?

Saudi riyal   [   ]

Indian rupees   [   ]

US dollars   [   ]

Japanese yen   [   ]

What do I receive if I change £100?

Australian dollars   [   ]

Thai baht   [   ]

Working out

Collins
New
Primary
Maths

Name _____ Date _____

Equivalent fractions

● **Find equivalent fractions**

Write as many equivalent fractions as you can for these fractions.

a $\dfrac{1}{9}$ = ——— = ——— = ——— = ——— = ——— = ———

b $\dfrac{1}{8}$ = ——— = ——— = ——— = ——— = ——— = ———

c $\dfrac{1}{12}$ = ——— = ——— = ——— = ——— = ——— = ———

d $\dfrac{1}{15}$ = ——— = ——— = ——— = ——— = ——— = ———

Be careful. These fractions have a numerator greater than one!

e $\dfrac{3}{4}$ = ——— = ——— = ——— = ——— = ——— = ———

f $\dfrac{2}{3}$ = ——— = ——— = ——— = ——— = ——— = ———

g $\dfrac{3}{5}$ = ——— = ——— = ——— = ——— = ——— = ———

h $\dfrac{2}{10}$ = ——— = ——— = ——— = ——— = ——— = ———

Now make up some yourself.

i ⬚ = ——— = ——— = ——— = ——— = ——— = ———

j ⬚ = ——— = ——— = ——— = ——— = ——— = ———

k ⬚ = ——— = ——— = ——— = ——— = ——— = ———

l ⬚ = ——— = ——— = ——— = ——— = ——— = ———

Name _____ Date _____

What's the per cent?

● **Find percentages of numbers and quantities**

1 Work out the percentages. Show your working on the back of this sheet.

   a What is 50% of £9?

   b What is 25% of £12?

   c What is 10% of £3?   **g** What is 40% of £200?

   d What is 50% of 17 km?   **h** What is 90% of 180 km?

   e What is 75% of 21m?   **i** What is 10% of £24?

   f What is 20% of 1 hour?   **j** What is 10% of 108 m?

2 We asked 200 people what their favourite fruit was. 40% said strawberries, 21% said peaches, 7% said oranges, 12% said bananas, 10% said apples. The rest of the people asked could not decide.

   a What percentage of people could not decide?

   b How many people was that?

   c How many people liked strawberries best?

3 A football team play 20 games a season. This season they lost 30% of their games.

   a What percentage of their games did they win?

   b How many games did they win?

   c How many games did they lose?

   d Next season they aim to win 90% of their games. How many games will that be?

Collins New Primary Maths

Name _____ Date _____

Chocolate boxes

● **Solve problems involving proportions of quantities**

1 In this box of chocolates, for every 1 white chocolate, there are 4 milk chocolates.

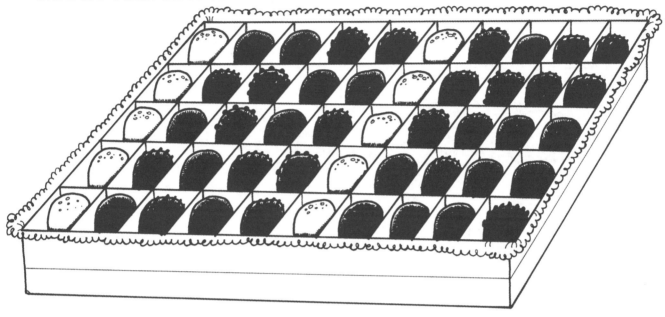

Answer these questions. Show all your working.

a How many white chocolates are there?

b How many milk chocolates are there?

c What fraction of the box is white chocolate?

d What fraction of the box is milk chocolate?

e What percentage of the box is white chocolate?

f What percentage of the box is milk chocolate?

2 Answer the questions again. This time, the proportion of white to milk chocolates is 2 : 3. Write your answers on the back of this sheet.

© HarperCollinsPublishers Ltd 2008

Name _____ Date _____

Checkout totals

- **Solve problems involving money**

1 Look at how much these items cost.
Copy and complete the shopping bills.

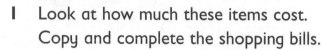

57p £1.25 £4 8p £1.60

£3.20 90p £5.36 per kg £1.29 per 100g Lamb

a

	cost
3 cakes	_____
2 loaves	_____
Orange juice	_____
Oatabix	_____
Chicken	_____
Washing powder	_____
Carrier bag	_____
Total	_____

b

	cost
2 orange juice	_____
Oatabix	_____
2 cakes	_____
200g lamb	_____
500g cheese	_____
3 carrier bags	_____
Total	_____

c

	cost
3 Oatabix	_____
2 orange juice	_____
Cake	_____
Washing powder	_____
Chicken	_____
4 loaves	_____
300g lamb	_____
250g cheese	_____
Total	_____

2 Use the shopping list on the right to calculate these costs.

a A box of eggs [ ]

b A can of drink [ ]

c 1 kg of potatoes [ ]

d 100 g of sausages [ ]

e A pack of butter [ ]

f 100 g of olives [ ]

g 400 g of sausages [ ]

h 2 kg of potatoes [ ]

i 3 cans of drink [ ]

j A box of tissues [ ]

Shopping List

3 boxes eggs	£2.55
6 cans drink	£2.10
5 kg potatoes	£1.85
200 g sausage	£2.54
4 packs butter	£4.48
50 g olives	62p
box tissues	
Total	£15.19

102

Name _____ Date _____

Helpful doubles

● **Use doubling to multiply by 12, 14, 16 and 18**

You need:

● 40 counters (20 of one colour, 20 of another)

● paper clip

● pencil and paper

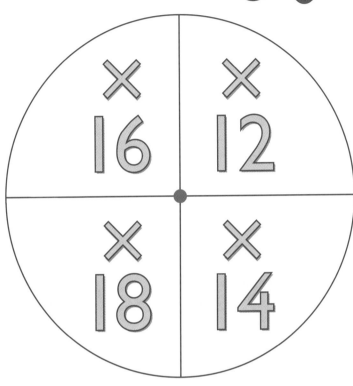

A game for 2 players.

● Take turns to choose a number from the balls, spin the spinner and perform the calculation.

● If the answer appears on the grid, cover it with one of your counters. If the number is already covered, miss a turn.

● The winner is the first player to complete a row, column or diagonal of 4 numbers.

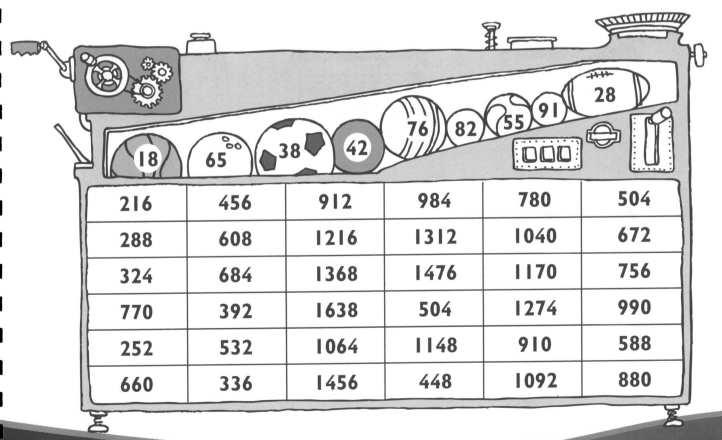

216	456	912	984	780	504
288	608	1216	1312	1040	672
324	684	1368	1476	1170	756
770	392	1638	504	1274	990
252	532	1064	1148	910	588
660	336	1456	448	1092	880

Name _____ Date _____

Calculator counting

● **Develop calculator skills and use a calculator effectively**

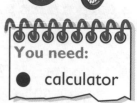

Starting at the numbers below, count on 5 steps.

Then use the constant function on your calculator to check.

1 For these numbers, count forwards in 1s.

a

386 400

b

472 363

c

501 277

d

652 526

e

700 638

f

167 998

You need:
● calculator

2 For these numbers, count forwards in 2s.

a

600 000

b

127 326

c

486 157

d

106 173

e

873 568

f

437 991

3 Check your answers on your calculator.

© Collins
New
Primary
Maths

Name _____ Date _____

Thousands order

- Explain what a digit represents in whole numbers and partition, round and order these numbers

1 Write these numbers out in order, from smallest to largest.

5367	2576	7584	3847	2394
5921	2493	8301	1075	5362

smallest

largest

2 Write the next number.

a 2561 [   ]   b 3795 [   ]   c 4732 [   ]

d 1093 [   ]   e 2197 [   ]   f 7521 [   ]

g 8280 [   ]   h 3075 [   ]   i 4762 [   ]

3 Write the previous number.

a [   ] 1065   b [   ] 2483   c [   ] 6278

d [   ] 5671   e [   ] 9203   f [   ] 4163

g [   ] 7241   h [   ] 3584   i [   ] 4853

4 Write the number that is 100 more.

a 4693 [   ]   b 1324 [   ]   c 4685 [   ]

d 3657 [   ]   e 2079 [   ]   f 6325 [   ]

g 5874 [   ]   h 3590 [   ]   i 1094 [   ]

Name _____ Date _____

Repeating calculations

● **Develop calculator skills and use a calculator effectively**

1 Calculate each answer.

Repeat the calculation to check your answer.

Circle the correct answers.

	First answer	**Second answer**
a £4.97 + £2.84		
b £3.52 + £1.84		
c 75p + 75p + 64p		
d £4.69 × 2		
e £28.52 + £39.47		
f £98.41 − £63.28		
g 23 × £1.74		
h £5.00 − £2.31		

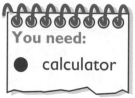

You need:
● calculator

2 Answer these questions using your calculator.

Check your answers by repeating the calculation.

Circle the correct answers.

	First answer	**Second answer**
a Find the total cost.		

£3·94 £4·21

| **b** How much do three pairs of scissors cost? | | |

£1·83

| **c** How much more expensive is the toy truck than the car? | |

£7·25

£8·63

 Collins New Primary Maths

Name _____ Date _____

More multiplication methods

- **Use efficient written methods for HTU × U, TU × TU and U.t × U**

For each calculation, approximate the answer first, then use the grid to work out the answer.

a 452 × 7 ○○

×	400	50	2
7			

= ☐

b 267 × 4 ○○

×	200	60	7
4			

= ☐

c 864 × 8 ○○

×			

= ☐

d 9·6 × 6 ○○

×	9·0	0·6
6		

= ☐

e 7·3 × 9 ○○

×	7·0	0·3
9		

= ☐

f 6·5 × 7 ○○

×		

= ☐

g 86 × 73 ○○

×	80	6
70		
3		

= ☐

h 55 × 92 ○○

×	50	5
90		
2		

= ☐

i 68 × 34 ○○

×		

= ☐

© HarperCollinsPublishers Ltd 2008

Name _____ Date _____

Recording division

● **Refine and use efficient written methods for HTU ÷ U**

1   Work out the answers to these in your head.

70 ÷ 7 =	150 ÷ 5 =	270 ÷ 3 =
60 ÷ 6 =	210 ÷ 7 =	360 ÷ 6 =
80 ÷ 4 =	320 ÷ 8 =	480 ÷ 8 =
60 ÷ 3 =	630 ÷ 9 =	420 ÷ 7 =
100 ÷ 5 =	480 ÷ 6 =	360 ÷ 4 =
120 ÷ 6 =	240 ÷ 4 =	540 ÷ 9 =

2   For each calculation, approximate the answer first.
   Then use a standard written method of division to record your work.

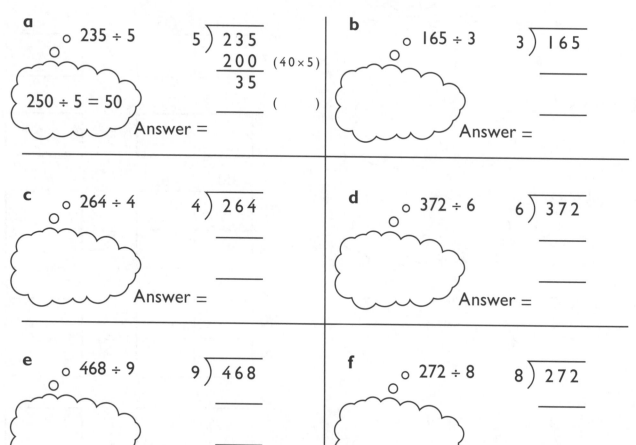

a   ○ 235 ÷ 5

250 ÷ 5 = 50

5) 235
    200   (40 × 5)
    ‾‾‾‾
     35
    ____ (   )
   Answer =

b   ○ 165 ÷ 3

3) 165
   ____

   ____
   Answer =

c   ○ 264 ÷ 4

4) 264
   ____

   ____
   Answer =

d   ○ 372 ÷ 6

6) 372
   ____

   ____
   Answer =

e   ○ 468 ÷ 9

9) 468
   ____

   ____
   Answer =

f   ○ 272 ÷ 8

8) 272
   ____

   ____
   Answer =

Collins New Primary Maths

Name _____ Date _____

Decimals in a row

● Explain what each digit represents in decimal numbers with up to two places

You need:

● 2 × 0-9 dice

● 2 different coloured pens

I rolled a 6 and a 3. I can make 0·63 or 0·36.

A game for 2 players.

● Take turns to roll both dice.

● Look at the two digits on the dice and use them to make a decimal to two places.

● Write the decimal number on the number line in your colour pen.

● The winner is the first person to get three decimal numbers in a row.

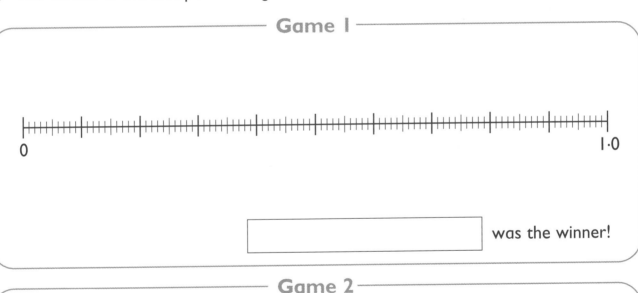

──── Game 1 ────

0   1·0

[   ] was the winner!

──── Game 2 ────

0   1·0

[   ] was the winner!

Name _____ Date _____

Healthy prices

● **Solve one-step and two-step problems involving whole numbers and decimals, choosing and using appropriate calculation strategies**

The health food shop prices everything per kilogram.

SUNFLOWER SEEDS £3·20 PER KILO

SULTANAS £3·70 PER KILO

RAISINS £2·20 PER KILO

PORRIDGE OATS £1·90 PER KILO

DRIED APRICOTS £2·80 PER KILO

Work out how much my shopping is going to cost me. Show all your working.

200 g of raisins

300 g of sultanas

700 g of porridge oats

150 g of sunflower seeds

450 g of dried apricots

Collins New Primary Maths

Name _____ Date _____

More multiplication methods

● **Use efficient written methods for HTU × U, TU × TU and U.t × U**

1   Approximate the answer to each calculation.

a

22 × 33

b

55 × 37

c

31 × 27

d

24 × 16

e
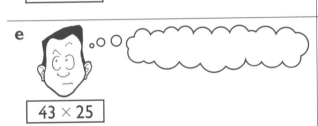
43 × 25

f

32 × 19

2   For each calculation above, work out the answer using a standard method of recording. Check your answer is close to your approximation.

a   **d**

b   **e**

c   **f**

Name _____ Date _____

Division methods

● **Refine and use efficient written methods for HTU ÷ U**

For each calculation approximate the answer first, then work out the answer using a standard written method of division.

Check your answer using the short standard method. Look at the worked example.

a   approximately

$5\ 2\ 7 \div 6 \rightarrow 5\ 4\ 0 \div 6 = 9\ 0$

```
          8 7 R 5
6)5 2 7        6)5 2 7
  4 8 0  (80 × 6)  4 8
    4 7             4 7
    4 2  (7 × 6)    4 2
     5               5
```

Answer = 8 7 R 5

b   approximately

$6\ 8\ 6 \div 9 \rightarrow$

c   approximately

$8\ 5\ 2 \div 7 \rightarrow$

d   approximately

$6\ 3\ 5 \div 5 \rightarrow$

e   approximately

$7\ 6\ 3 \div 4 \rightarrow$

f   approximately

$4\ 9\ 8 \div 3 \rightarrow$

Collins
New
Primary
Maths

Name _____ Date _____

Subtraction using the written method without borrowing

● **Use efficient written methods to subtract whole numbers**

I Write these calculations vertically and then work them out using the standard method. Be sure to make an estimate first. Write it in the cloud.

a 356 − 135

b 647 − 421

c 638 − 216

d 465 − 104

e 738 − 434

f 666 − 345

g 844 − 331

h 976 − 861

i 873 − 531

2 This calculation has been laid out using the expanded method.
Look at it and use it to help you explain how the written method works.

```
743 − 531 = 212

      700    40    3
    − 500    30    1
      ─────────────
      200    10    2
```

© HarperCollinsPublishers Ltd 2008

Collins
New
Primary
Maths

113

Name _____ Date _____

Problem solving using a calculator

● Use a calculator to solve problems, including those involving decimals

1 Enter these amounts of money into the calculator and then press the equals button. Write down what is in the display.

a £3.40

b £2.70

c £8.20

2 Look at these numbers that were displayed on a calculator. How would you write them if they were the answer to a money calculation?

a 5·2

b 2·8

c 16·7

3 Use your calculator to work out the answers to these calculations. Write the answer the calculator shows in the box. Write the answer in pounds and pence in the oval.

a £1.90 + £7.60

b £9.50 + £8.40

c £6.40 + £2.60

4 I save £1.30 every week.

a How much will I save in 4 weeks?

b How much will I save in 7 weeks?

c If I have saved £15.60, how many weeks did that take me?

d If I have saved £19.50, how many weeks did that take me?

I put in £3.60 but the calculator shows 3·6!

5 Why doesn't the calculator show the 0 in amounts of money that are multiples of 10p?

Remainders as fractions

- **Express a quotient as a fraction when dividing whole numbers**

The children in class 5 had a pizza party as their end of year celebration. The children sat in groups determined by the flavour pizza they liked best.

Work out how many whole pizzas each group received.

Divide the remaining pizzas by the number of groups to find out what fraction of the remaining pizza each group received.

10 pizzas
4 groups

Number of pizzas = $10 \div 4 = 2\frac{2}{4}$
= $2\frac{1}{2}$ pizzas per group

Mushroom
_____

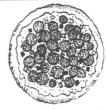

13 pizzas

2 groups

Pepperoni
_____

17 pizzas

4 groups

Tuna and sweetcorn
_____

11 pizzas

5 groups

Cheese and tomato
_____

21 pizzas

4 groups

Spicy beef

Collins
New
Primary
Maths

Name _____ Date _____

Multiplication and division mixed bag

- **Use known facts and place value to multiply and divide mentally**

Work out the answer to each calculation.

1

× 10
× 100
Lucky dip

a 4 × 200 =

b 3 × 500 =

c 6 × 300 =

d 40 × 200 =

e 30 × 500 =

f 60 × 300 =

2

÷ 10
÷ 100
÷ 1000
Lucky dip

a 3500 ÷ 10 =

b 6200 ÷ 100 =

c 7600 ÷ 10 =

d 7000 ÷ 1000 =

e 4000 ÷ 1000 =

f 3900 ÷ 100 =

3

Doubles
Lucky dip

a 430 × 2 =

b 4·6 × 2 =

c 6·5 × 2 =

d 2·8 × 2 =

e 380 × 2 =

f 435 × 2 =

4

Halves
Lucky dip

a 680 ÷ 2 =

b 0·72 ÷ 2 =

c 0·84 ÷ 2 =

d 840 ÷ 2 =

e 900 ÷ 2 =

f 460 ÷ 2 =

5

× 2 × 3
× 4 × 5
Lucky dip

a 26 × 3 =

b 34 × 4 =

c 53 × 5 =

d 67 × 2 =

e 39 × 4 =

f 48 × 3 =

Collins
New
Primary
Maths

Name _____Date _____

Net of a triangular prism

● **Draw nets of 3-D shapes**

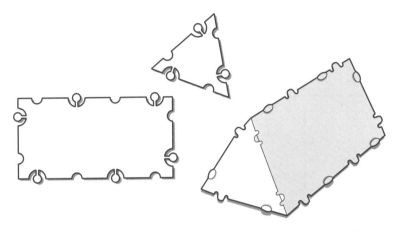

You need:

● 2 equilateral triangle interlocking tiles

● 3 rectangle interlocking tiles

● ruler ● scissors

● glue

1 Construct a triangular prism from the interlocking tiles.

2 Complete the net of the triangular prism on this grid and then add tabs to your drawing.

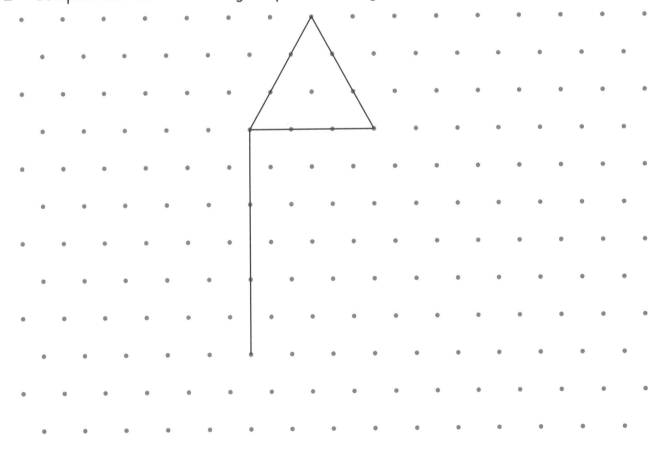

3 Carefully cut out your net and glue the tabs in one piece.
Fold up the net to make a triangular prism.

Name _____ Date _____

Triangle overlaps

● **Use properties to identify and draw 2-D shapes**

1 ● Translate each triangle 1 unit to the right.

   ● Colour the overlap.

   ● Name the shape in the overlap.

You need:
● coloured pencils   ● ruler

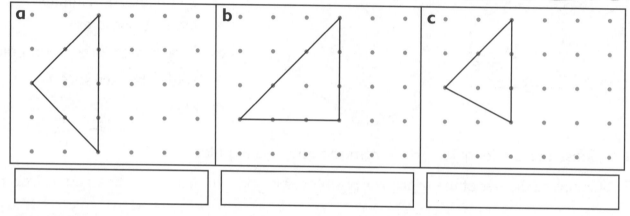

2 ● Translate each triangle 1 unit to the right, then 1 unit up.

   ● Colour the overlap.

   ● Name the shape in the overlap.

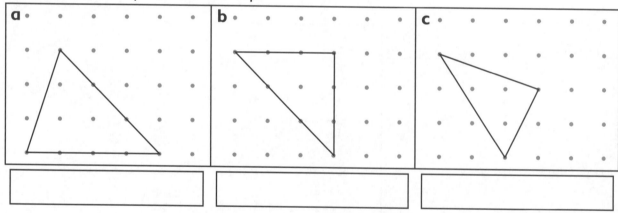

3 Draw a triangle in each grid. Repeat the steps in question **2**.

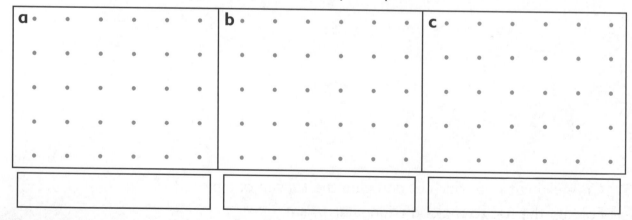

Collins New Primary Maths

Name _____ Date _____

Missing numbers

● **Use efficient written methods to add whole numbers**

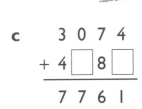

Fill in the missing numbers.

Don't forget to think about the numbers that were carried!

a
```
   2 6 8 4
+  5 8 0 □
   8 4 9 1
     | |
```

b
```
  □ 9 6 3
+ 3 0 7 □
  9 0 3 8
    | |
```

c
```
  3 0 7 4
+ 4 □ 8 □
  7 7 6 1
    | |
```

d
```
  □ 8 7 4
+ 5 2 □ 6
  9 0 9 0
    | |
```

e
```
  7 3 □ 2
+ □ 2 9 7
1 1 6 3 9
      |
```

f
```
  4 0 7 2
+ 3 □ 0 □
  7 5 8 0
      |
```

g
```
  □ 6 2 8
+ 4 9 7 □
1 0 6 0 0
    | | |
```

h
```
  8 6 □ 5
+ □ 0 7 5
1 0 7 4 0
      | |
```

i
```
  6 4 □ 4
+ □ 8 9 2
1 0 3 1 6
    | |
```

j
```
  8 6 2 □
+ □ 7 2 1
1 8 3 4 5
    |
```

k
```
  9 5 □ 2
+ □ 2 8 3
1 4 8 4 5
      |
```

l
```
  8 4 2 □
+ 5 □ 8 6
1 3 7 1 3
    | |
```

m
```
  □ 8 2 □
+  4 6 1 7
1 2 4 4 6
    | |
```

n
```
  8 5 1 □
+ 8 □ 9 4
1 6 8 1 1
    | |
```

o
```
  9 3 □ 9
+ □ 5 7 0
1 5 9 5 9
      |
```

Collins New Primary Maths

Name _____ Date _____

Shopping bills

● **Use efficient written methods to add whole numbers and decimals**

Add up these shopping bills. Then check your answers using a calculator. If your answer is wrong, see if you can work out where you made your mistake.

You need:
● calculator

SUPA!SHOP
100 High St. Hexingham
09:44   25-07-07
£3.15
£12.87
£5.74
£27.63

SUPA!SHOP
100 High St. Hexingham
12:11   07-09-07
£12.99
£36.53
£7.68
£11.59
£0.55

SUPA!SHOP
100 High St Hexingham
14:50 07-12-07
£10.41
£4.16
£20.66
£32.44
£17.39

Name _____ Date _____

Rounding remainders

● **Round up or down after division, depending on the context**

1 Read each word problem. There is a remainder in each situation.
Determine whether the answer will need to be rounded up or down.
Draw an arrow ↑ (up) or ↓ (down) by each problem.

a ☐ people are waiting for the
train. One carriage holds
☐ people. How many
carriages are needed in total? ◯

b I have £ ☐ . A train ticket to
London costs £ ☐ per day.
How many days can I travel? ◯

c There are ☐ children in Acorn
Primary School. They are travelling
by coach to the seaside. Each
coach seats ☐ children. How
many coaches were needed? ◯

d There are ☐ packed lunches to
take on the trip. One box holds
☐ lunches. How many boxes
are needed in total? ◯

e Joanne is going on holiday. The air
ticket costs £ ☐ . Joanne saves
£ ☐ per month. How many
months must she save until she has
enough money for a ticket? ◯

f There are ☐ taxi cabs. ☐
people are in the queue. Each cab
takes ☐ passengers.
How many cabs are full? ◯

g Petrol costs £ ☐ per litre. I have
£ ☐ to spend.
How many litres can I buy? ◯

2 Complete your own examples by filling in appropriate numbers to check
if you are correct. Write the answers in the oval.

Name _____ Date _____

Multiplication and division mixed bag

- **Use known facts and place value to multiply and divide mentally**

Work out the answer to each calculation.

1

×10
×100
Lucky Dip

a 50 × 300 = ☐   **b** 400 × 60 = ☐

c 80 × 70 = ☐   **d** 600 × 900 = ☐

e 900 × 70 = ☐   **f** 700 × 40 = ☐

2

÷10
÷100
÷1000
Lucky Dip

a 6300 ÷ 10 = ☐   **b** 9100 ÷ 100 = ☐

c 7800 ÷ 100 = ☐   **d** 96 000 ÷ 1000 = ☐

e 8000 ÷ 10 = ☐   **f** 6000 ÷ 1000 = ☐

3

Doubles
Lucky Dip

a 495 × 2 = ☐   **b** 6·7 × 2 = ☐

c 674 × 2 = ☐   **d** 2 × 8·9 = ☐

e 8·3 × 2 = ☐   **f** 2 × 515 = ☐

4

Halves
Lucky Dip

a 990 ÷ 2 = ☐   **b** 0·75 ÷ 2 = ☐   **c** 680 ÷ 2 = ☐

d 0·53 ÷ 2 = ☐   **e** 350 ÷ 2 = ☐   **f** 740 ÷ 2 = ☐

5

×4 ×6
×7 ×9
Lucky Dip

a 500 × 9 = ☐   **b** 85 × 4 = ☐   **c** 800 × 7 = ☐

d 58 × 7 = ☐   **e** 700 × 6 = ☐   **f** 66 × 4 = ☐

Collins
New
Primary
Maths

Name _____ Date _____

Cross-pentomino puzzle

● Investigate a general statement about familiar shapes by finding examples that satisfy it

You can make this cross using all twelve pentominoes.

Four pentominoes, P, V, W and X are shown in their correct positions.

1 Cut out the remaining eight pentominoes from the bottom of the sheet.

2 Find a way to cover the rest of the surface of the cross with these eight pentominoes.

3 When you have solved the puzzle, glue the pentominoes in position.

You need:
● scissors
● glue

Name _____ Date _____

Overlapping kites

● **Use properties to identify and draw 2-D shapes**

1 Find different arrangements for pairs of overlapping identical kites.

2 Name the shape created by the overlap each time.

You can translate, rotate or
reflect the kite shape.

You need:

● coloured
  pencils

● ruler

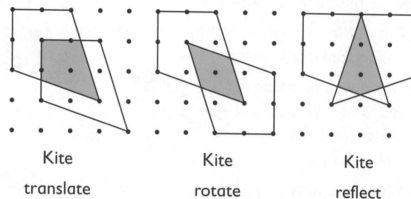

Kite	Kite	Kite
translate	rotate	reflect

© HarperCollinsPublishers Ltd 2008

Collins
New
Primary
Maths

Name _____ Date _____

Domino litres

● **Use, read and write standard metric units of capacity**

An activity for two players.

Equivalent dominoes match.

You need:

● scissors

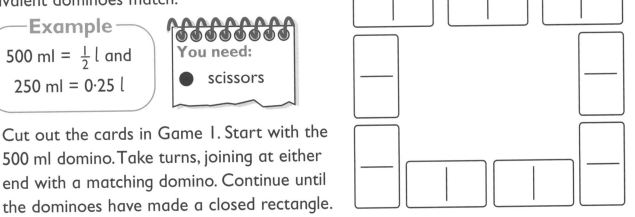

1 Cut out the cards in Game 1. Start with the 500 ml domino. Take turns, joining at either end with a matching domino. Continue until the dominoes have made a closed rectangle.

2 Choose a different starting domino and make a new rectangle.

3 Cut out the cards for Game 2 and play as before.

Game 1

$\frac{4}{5}$ l	$\frac{3}{10}$ l	100 ml
$\frac{2}{5}$ l	750 ml	$\frac{1}{5}$ l
400 ml	$\frac{3}{4}$ l	200 ml
$\frac{3}{5}$ l	500 ml	$\frac{1}{4}$ l
600 ml	$\frac{1}{2}$ l	250 ml
$\frac{1}{10}$ l	800 ml	300 ml

Game 2

800 ml	300 ml	0·1 l
400 ml	0·75 l	200 ml
0·4 l	750 ml	0·2 l
600 ml	0·5 l	250 ml
0·6 l	500 ml	0·25 l
100 ml	0·8 l	0·3 l

Name _____ Date _____

River level line graphs

● **Use line graphs to answer questions**

1 The diagrams show the depth of river levels in metres. The levels are shown at the start of each month. Complete the table on the right.

You need:
● ruler

Month	Depth (metres)
January	
February	
March	
April	
May	
June	
July	
August	
September	
October	
November	
December	

January February March April

May June July August

September October November December

2 Use a ruler to complete the line graph.

3 a What was the depth in July?

b When was the depth 6 metres?

c What was the greatest depth?

d When was the water level lowest? Explain why.

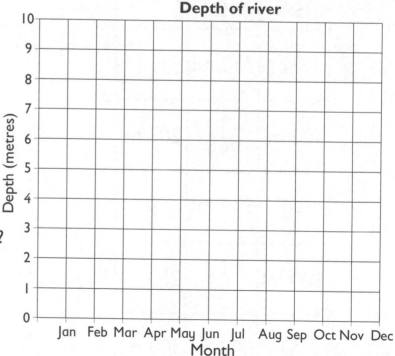

Depth of river

Month

Collins
New
Primary
Maths

Name _____ Date _____

Blimps

● **Use time–distance graphs to answer questions**

Jameela sent her radio-controlled blimp on a journey.

You need:
● ruler

The graph shows the height of the blimp at various times.

1 How high was the blimp after:

a 2 seconds

b 6 seconds

c 1 second?

2 When was the blimp

a 12 metres high

b 6 metres high?

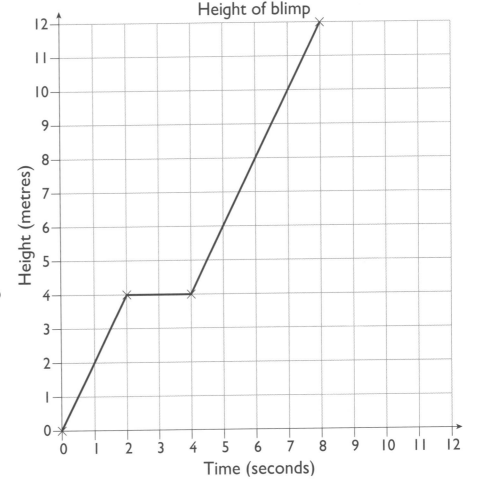

The blimp started to come down after 8 seconds.

3 It was 6 metres high after 10 seconds. Mark this point on the graph. Join this point to the graph with a straight line.

4 The blimp landed after 12 seconds. Mark this point on the graph. Join this point to the graph with a straight line.

Name _____ Date _____

Treadmill

- **Use graphs to answer questions**

Stephanie spent 15 minutes running on her treadmill.

Stephanie's heart rate on the treadmill

Heart rate (beats per minutes) vs *Time (minutes)*

The graph shows her heart rate whilst exercising.

1 What was her heart rate just as she started running?

2 What was her heart rate after 3 minutes on the treadmill?

You need:
- ruler

3 When was her heart rate:

a 80 beats per minute

b 100 beats per minute?

4 a What happened after 6 minutes of running?

b Why do you think this happened?

5 How long did it take for her heart rate to rise to 110 beats per minute?

6 When did Stephanie run the fastest?

7 Stephanie left the treadmill after 15 minutes.
Her heart rate was 95 beats per minute. Draw a line to complete the line graph.

128

© HarperCollins*Publishers* Ltd 2008

Collins
New
Primary
Maths

Name _____ Date _____

Trominoes

● **Use, read and write standard metric units of capacity**

Equivalent trominoes match,
for example 0·5 l = 500 ml = $\frac{1}{2}$ l

You need:
● scissors

● Cut out the 12 trominoes.

● Place them face down on the table, shuffle and take 6 trominoes each.

● The player with the 500 ml tromino begins.

● Take turns, joining to a tromino which shows an equivalent capacity.

● If you cannot go, you miss a turn.

● The first to play all 6 cards is the winner.

A game for two players

Name _____ Date _____

Rising levels

● **Collect and organise data to find out about a subject**

1 Turn on the tap so that the jug will fill up slowly.

Place the 1 litre measuring jug underneath the tap and start the timer.

2 After 10 seconds, remove the jug and measure the level of the water using the jug scale. Keep the tap running.

Repeat until the jug is filled.

Record your measurements in a table.

3 Draw a line graph to show your results.

4 Place an object inside the jug and repeat steps 1 and 2.

If the object floats, hold it down with a pencil.

Before you start, try to predict what the graph will look like compared to your first graph.

5 Draw a second line graph to show your results.

6 Repeat, using objects with different shapes.

For each object, predict what the graph will look like.

You need:

● 1 litre measuring jug
● water running from tap
● stopwatch
● differently shaped heavy objects to place in jug
● graph paper
● ruler   ● pencil

130

Collins
New
Primary
Maths

Name _____ Date _____

Taxi line graphs

● **Use line graphs to answer questions**

Jim is a taxi driver. The table shows his journey one evening.

Place	Distance from home	Time
Home	0 miles	7:00 p.m.
Paxton Rd	5 miles	7:15 p.m.
Club	20 miles	7:45 p.m.
Station	25 miles	8:00 p.m.
Half hour tea break		8:30 p.m.
Hotel	35 miles	9:00 p.m.
Airport	50 miles	9:30 p.m.
15 min tea break		9:45 p.m.
Station	25 miles	10:15 p.m.
Home	0 miles	11:00 p.m.

1 a Where was Jim at 8:00 p.m.?

   b When did Jim stop for his second tea break?

   c Where was Jim when he was 40 miles from home?

   d How far is the airport from Jim's home?

   e How far is it from the club to the hotel?

   f How long did it take Jim to travel home from the station?

2 Complete this line graph for his journey.

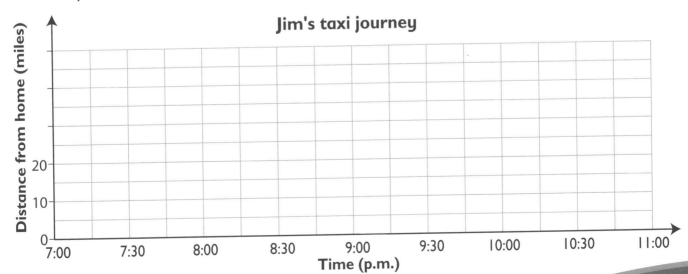

Jim's taxi journey

Name _____ Date _____

Wonky spinner

● Collect and organise data to answer a question
● Describe how likely an event is to happen

1   Look at the spinner. Are the
    numbers equally likely to happen?

    Why?

You need:
● paper clip
● pencil
● 1 cm squared
  paper or graph
  paper

2   Which numbers are
    equally likely to happen?

3   Write the letters A, B, C on the spinner
    so that A and B are equally likely. Every
    space must have a letter.

4   Write down the chance of the spinner landing on C.

5   Spin the spinner at least 50 times. Record your results in tally charts: one for the
    numbers, one for the letters.

6   Draw a chart for each set of data.

7   Are the results as you expected? Explain your answers.

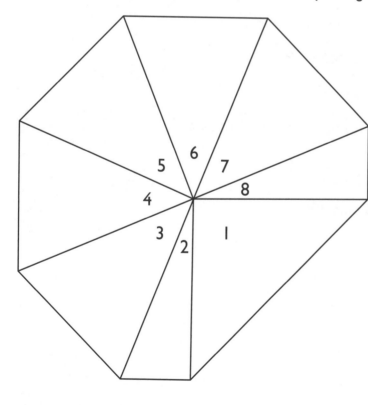

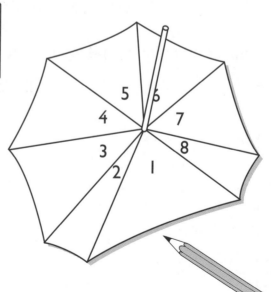

Collins
New
Primary
Maths

Name _____ Date _____

Money calculations

- **Use a calculator to solve problems**

1 Calculate each answer.
   Repeat the calculation to check your answer.

   Circle the correct answers.

You need:
- calculator

		First answer	**Second answer**
a	£6.85 + £1.34		
b	£4.25 – £2.42		
c	85p + 85p + 74p		
d	£3.96 × 3		
e	£82·14 + £64·74		
f	£26·41 – £25·52		
g	22 × £1·60		
h	£5.00 – £3.25		

2 Answer these questions using your calculator.
   Check your answers by repeating the calculation.

   Circle the correct answers.

First answer   **Second answer**

a Find the total cost.

£2.95

£5.31

b How much do three pens cost?

£2.73

c How much more expensive is the scarf?

£14.25   £5.92

Name _____ Date _____

Solving word problems

- ● **Solve word problems**

football
£35

netball
£24

rugby ball
£28

basketball
£16

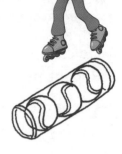

pack of 3
tennis balls £4

Read the word problems. Choose an appropriate method of calculating your answer:

- ● Mental
- ● Mental with jottings
- ● Paper and pencil

HINT
Show all your working

1 The sports shop sells 100 footballs and 100 netballs over the weekend. How much money did they take in sales?	**2** Buy one of each item. How much do you spend?	**3** How much does it cost to buy a total of 30 tennis balls?
4 Netballs cost £24. If you buy ten you save £20. How much does it cost for ten?	**5** Maria wants to buy 12 basketballs for her team. She has £200. Does she have enough money? 	**6** Buy 5 packs of tennis balls, get one pack FREE! If you spend £60, how many tennis balls will you have altogether? 

Collins
New
Primary
Maths

Name _____ Date _____

Marking in millilitres

● Display capacity on a measuring jug with unlabelled divisions

Draw a straight line to show the level of liquid in each measuring jug. Colour the liquid up to the line.

You need:
● coloured pencils   ● ruler

a

— 250 ml
— 200 ml
— 150 ml
— 100 ml
— 50 ml

50 ml

b

— 250 ml
— 200 ml
— 150 ml
— 100 ml
— 50 ml

130 ml

c

— 500 ml
— 400 ml
— 300 ml
— 200 ml
— 100 ml

275 ml

d

— 500 ml
— 400 ml
— 300 ml
— 200 ml
— 100 ml

350 ml

e

— 500 ml
— 400 ml
— 300 ml
— 200 ml
— 100 ml

460 ml

370 ml

f

— 500 ml
— 400 ml
— 300 ml
— 200 ml
— 100 ml

280 ml

g

— 1000 ml
— 800 ml
— 600 ml
— 400 ml
— 200 ml

900 ml

h

— 1000 ml
— 900 ml
— 800 ml
— 700 ml
— 600 ml
— 500 ml
— 400 ml
— 300 ml
— 200 ml
— 100 ml

Name _____ Date _____

Translating a shape

● **Use co-ordinates to translate a shape**

In each grid the first shape is plotted.

Follow the instructions to plot a second shape in each grid.

Join the points in order.
Then complete the sentence for each translation.

You need:
● ruler

Translate means slide or move in a straight line.

1 Plot these points to make shape B:
(4, 2) (6, 2) (5, 4)

Shape A has been translated

[   ] squares to the

[   ] to make shape B.

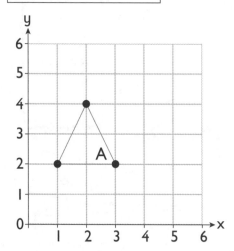

2 Plot these points to make shape D:
(4, 1) (6, 2) (3, 3)

Shape C has been translated

[   ] squares

[   ] to make shape D.

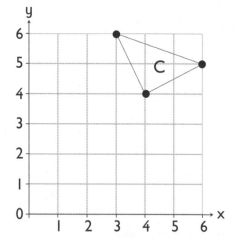

3 Plot these points to make shape F:
(0, 2) (2, 2) (2, 5) (0, 4)

Shape E has been translated

[   ] squares to the

[   ] to make shape F.

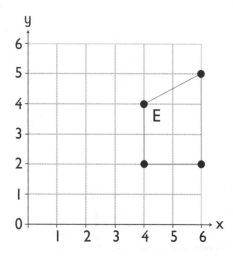

Collins
New Primary Maths

Name _____ Date _____

Fencing the vegetable garden

● **Solve one-step and two-step problems involving whole numbers**

Mr Green has been fencing his garden.

Here is part of his new fence.

a Each post is 12 cm wide.

The total length of this fence is 140 cm.

Both gaps are the same. How long is each gap?

Show all your working.

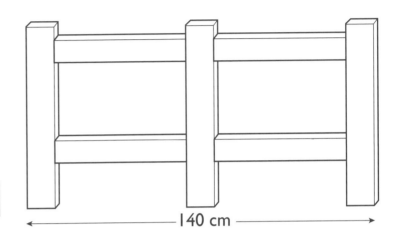

←———————— 140 cm ————————→

b Mr. Green's fence is rectangular in shape. If one of the other sides of Mr. Green's fence is 380 cm, what is the perimeter of his fence?

c What is the total area of Mr. Green's vegetable garden?

— **Working out** —

Name _____ Date _____

Rounding error

● **Develop calculator skills and use a calculator effectively**

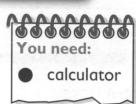

1 Work out each calculation using your calculator. Write the answer on your calculator display in the first box. Write the rounded answer in the second box.

You need:
● calculator

a 5 ÷ 12 × 6 =

b 14 ÷ 12 × 3 =

c 12·5 ÷ 3 × 6 =

d 6·25 ÷ 6 × 12 =

e 76 ÷ 24 × 3 =

f 7 ÷ 300 × 150 =

g 26 ÷ 72 × 18 =

h 5 ÷ 6000 × 3000 =

i 0·25 ÷ 18 × 36 =

j 7·5 ÷ 90 × 30 =

2 Work out the first part of each calculation using your calculator. Find the missing number that gives the answer. Choose from: 3, 6, 9, 12, 15, 18, or 30.

a 9 ÷ 6 × ☐ = 4·5

b 5 ÷ 18 × ☐ = 2·5

c 3·1 ÷ 6 × ☐ = 7·75

d 2·5 ÷ 3 × ☐ = 7·5

e 3·25 ÷ 6 × ☐ = 6·5

f 0·65 ÷ 3 × ☐ = 6·5

g 15·5 ÷ 3 × ☐ = 77·5

h 43·5 ÷ 18 × ☐ = 14·5

3 A full bottle of drink fills the number of cups shown. Find the amount contained in each individual cup.

a 500 ml

Maria fills 9 cups.
Amount in each cup =

b 700 ml

Jerry fills 15 cups.
Amount in each cup =

c 1000 ml

Peter fills 27 cups.
Amount in each cup =

d 2500 ml

Naomi fills 21 cups.
Amount in each cup =

Name _____ Date _____

Pegging out areas

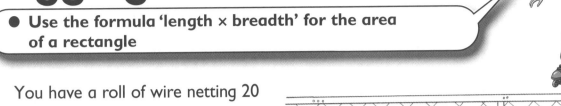

- **Use the formula 'length × breadth' for the area of a rectangle**

1 You have a roll of wire netting 20 metres long, 4 corner posts and a hammer to build a new rectangular enclosure for your pet rabbit.

You want to give the rabbit the largest possible area to run about in.

a Complete this table.

Length in metres	9	8	7	6	5	4	3	2	1
Breadth in metres	1	2							
Area in m^2	9								

b Write the dimensions of the rectangle which you will build.

Length [   ] m and breadth [   ] m

2 If you had a roll of wire netting 24 metres long, what is the largest possible area of run you can build?

Complete the table.

Length in metres	11	10	9	8	7	6	5	4	3
Breadth in metres	1	2							
Area in m^2	9								

Answer: [   ]

3 There is a hole in the netting.

You only have 16 metres.

On the back of the sheet, draw the rectangle you would build with the largest possible area.

Name _____ Date _____

Geometric designs

● Complete symmetrical patterns with two lines of symmetry at right angles

The Sioux and Cheyenne tribes of Plains Indians used the 'hour glass' design for decoration of tepees, moccasins and pouches. To contrast with the colour of buffalo hide, they only used five colours: red, yellow, blue, white and black.

You need:
● red, yellow, blue and black pencils

1 Using the axes of symmetry, complete the geometric design.

2 Colour the regions of the design to show its reflective symmetry.

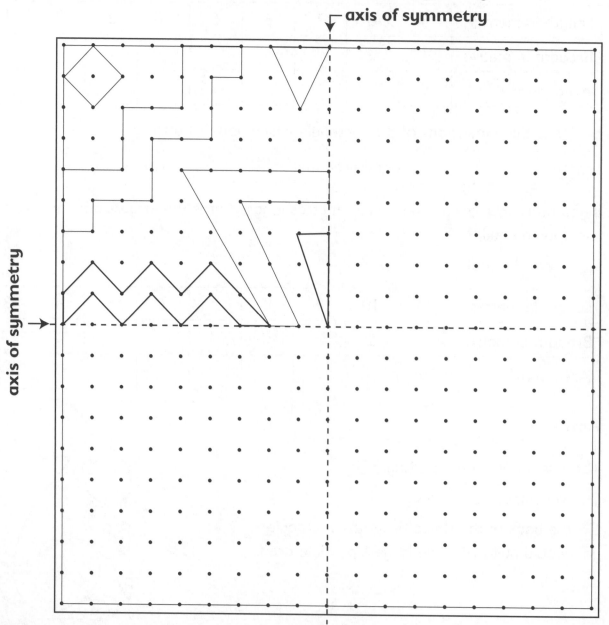

Name _____ Date _____

Calculator fractions

- **Relate fractions to division, and use division to find simple fractions**

Use the calculator to find these fractions.

For some of them the calculation you need to do on the calculator has been written for you.

You need:
- calculator

a $\frac{1}{4}$ of 48   =   12

    48 ÷ 4   =   12

b $\frac{1}{3}$ of 36   =   ☐

    36 ÷ 3   =   ☐

c $\frac{1}{5}$ of 65   =   ☐

    65 ÷ 5   =   ☐

d $\frac{1}{10}$ of 120 = ☐

    120 ÷ 10 = ☐

e $\frac{1}{4}$ of 52   =   ☐

    52 ÷ ☐ = ☐

f $\frac{1}{6}$ of 78   =   ☐

    78 ÷ ☐ = ☐

g $\frac{1}{5}$ of 80   =   ☐

    ☐ ÷ ☐ = ☐

h $\frac{1}{3}$ of 45   =   ☐

    ☐ ÷ ☐ = ☐

i $\frac{1}{4}$ of 68   =   ☐

    ☐ ÷ ☐ = ☐

j $\frac{1}{10}$ of 160 = ☐

    ☐ ÷ ☐ = ☐

k $\frac{1}{6}$ of 84   =   ☐

    ☐ ÷ ☐ = ☐

l $\frac{1}{3}$ of 42   =   ☐

    ☐ ÷ ☐ = ☐

Collins New Primary Maths

Name _____ Date _____

Equal fractions and decimals

You need:
● coloured pencils

● **Relate fractions to their decimal equivalents**

Shade in the following fractions of each shape, then write the equivalent decimal.

a

$\dfrac{1}{4}$

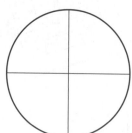

The equivalent decimal is [____].

b

$\dfrac{3}{4}$

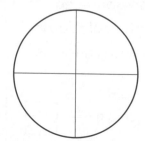

The equivalent decimal is [____].

c

$\dfrac{1}{10}$

The equivalent decimal is [____].

d

$\dfrac{7}{10}$

The equivalent decimal is [____].

e

$\dfrac{4}{10}$

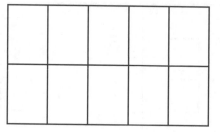

The equivalent decimal is [____].

f

$\dfrac{5}{10}$

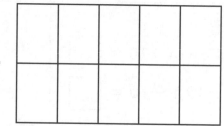

The equivalent decimal is [____].

g

$\dfrac{30}{100}$

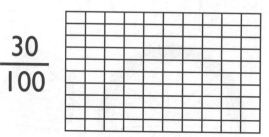

The equivalent decimal is [____].

h

$\dfrac{80}{100}$

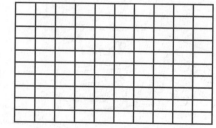

The equivalent decimal is [____].

Collins
New
Primary
Maths

Name _____ Date _____

Percentages

● **Understand percentage as the number of parts in every 100**

1 Shade the grid in the following percentages and colours.

a 50% red

b 10% blue

c 5% yellow

d 25% green

e 10% orange

You need:

● red, blue, yellow, green and orange coloured pencils

Remember the whole grid is 100%

1%	1%	1%	1%	1%	1%	1%	1%	1%	1%
1%	1%	1%	1%	1%	1%	1%	1%	1%	1%
1%	1%	1%	1%	1%	1%	1%	1%	1%	1%
1%	1%	1%	1%	1%	1%	1%	1%	1%	1%
1%	1%	1%	1%	1%	1%	1%	1%	1%	1%
1%	1%	1%	1%	1%	1%	1%	1%	1%	1%
1%	1%	1%	1%	1%	1%	1%	1%	1%	1%
1%	1%	1%	1%	1%	1%	1%	1%	1%	1%
1%	1%	1%	1%	1%	1%	1%	1%	1%	1%
1%	1%	1%	1%	1%	1%	1%	1%	1%	1%

2 Now answer these questions.

a What per cent of the grid is red and blue?

b What per cent of the grid is orange and yellow?

c What per cent of the grid is shaded?

d What per cent of the grid is not red?

Name _____ Date _____

Proportion problems

● Solve simple problems involving proportions

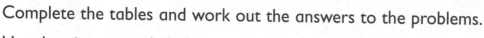

Complete the tables and work out the answers to the problems.
Use the pictures to help you.

1. I have made some cakes. For every one chocolate cake, I have made two currant cakes. If I have made five chocolate cakes, how many currant cakes have I made?

Chocolate	Currant
1	2

2. When we eat sweets I eat one and my brother eats three. If I ate six, how many would my brother have eaten?

Me	My brother
1	

3. For every five packets of crisps, one has a sticker in it and four do not. I have bought 25 packets of crisps. How many stickers will I have?

Sticker	No sticker
1	4

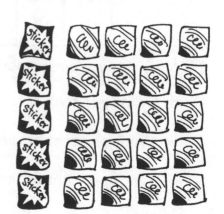

Collins
New
Primary
Maths

Name _____ Date _____

Reviewing written multiplication and division

● Use efficient written methods to multiply and divide
HTU × U, TU × TU, U.t × U and HTU ÷ U

1 For each multiplication calculation, approximate the answer first and write it in the bubble. Then use the grid to work out the answer.

a 387 × 8 ∘ ∘ ○

×	300	80	7	
8				=

b 684 × 6 ∘ ∘ ○

×				
				=

c 6·7 × 5 ∘ ∘ ○

×	6·0	0·7	
5			=

d 8·3 × 8 ∘ ∘ ○

×			
			=

e 93 × 47 ∘ ∘ ○

×	90	3	
40			
7			=

f 58 × 76 ∘ ∘ ○

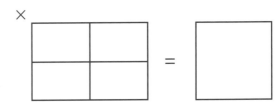

×			
			=

2 For each division calculation, approximate the answer first and write it in the bubble. Then work out the answer.

a 445 ÷ 6

b 675 ÷ 8

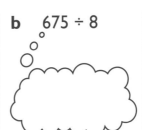

Name _____ Date _____

Number patterns

● **Explain a generalised relationship in words**

● Continue each pattern.

● Write an addition calculation for each pattern.

● Continue the pattern on the back of this sheet until you reach the 15th sequence in the pattern. (You may need more paper.)

1

2

1 + 2 = ☐

2 + 4 = ☐

1 + 2 + 3 = ☐

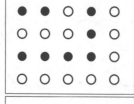

2 + 4 + 6 = ☐

Name _____ Date _____

What's the fraction?

● **Relate fractions to division, and use division to find simple fractions**

Answer these problems. Use the space below for your working.

I I buy 1 litre of water. I drink 400 ml and then spill some. There is 100 ml left.

  a What fraction did I drink? ⬜

  b What fraction did I spill? ⬜

2 In one day I work for 8 hours and sleep for 10 hours.

  a What fraction of the day did I sleep? ⬜

  b What fraction of the day did I work? ⬜

3 I have £10. I spend £7.50.

  a What fraction did I spend? ⬜

  b What fraction do I have left? ⬜

4 My journey to school is 1 km. I walk on my own for 700 m and with a friend for 300 m.

  a What fraction of the journey am I on my own? ⬜

  b What fraction of the journey am I with a friend? ⬜

5 I spend one hour on my homework. Reading a chapter of my book takes 25 minutes and maths takes me 35 minutes.

  a What fraction of the time do I spend reading? ⬜

  b What fraction of the time do I spend on maths? ⬜

6 I am going on holiday and my case weighs 18 kg. 6 kg is shoes, and the rest is clothes.

  a What fraction of the weight is shoes? ⬜

  b What fraction of the weight is clothes? ⬜

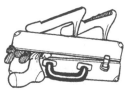

Name _____ Date _____

Match the numbers

● **Relate fractions to their decimal equivalents**

Cut up the cards and shuffle them. You must match the fraction with the equivalent decimal. Play Pairs or Snap with a partner.

You need:
● scissors

Pairs
● Place all the cards out on the table face down.
● Take turns to choose two cards.
● If they are an equivalent fraction and decimal, keep them. If not, put them back in the same position.
● The player with the most pairs is the winner.

Snap
● Deal the cards out between the two players.
● Take turns to place a card on the table face up.
● When there are two cards with an equivalent fraction and decimal, the first player to shout 'snap' takes all the cards.
● Play until one player holds all the cards.

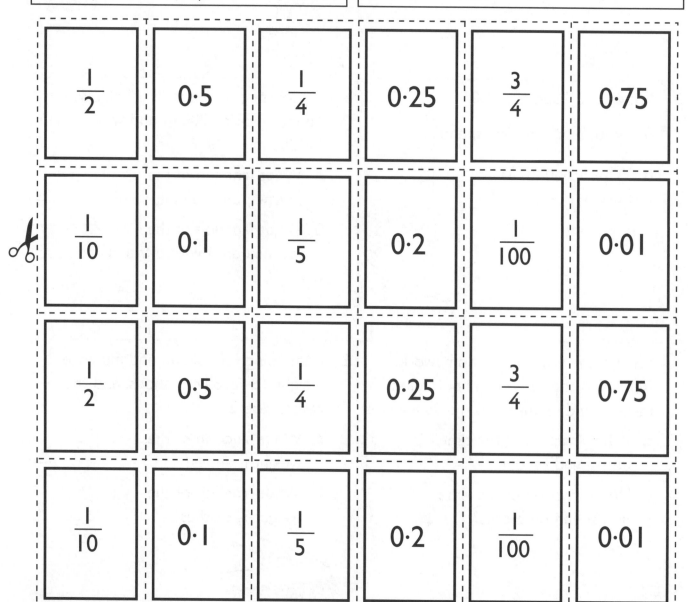

$\frac{1}{2}$	0·5	$\frac{1}{4}$	0·25	$\frac{3}{4}$	0·75
$\frac{1}{10}$	0·1	$\frac{1}{5}$	0·2	$\frac{1}{100}$	0·01
$\frac{1}{2}$	0·5	$\frac{1}{4}$	0·25	$\frac{3}{4}$	0·75
$\frac{1}{10}$	0·1	$\frac{1}{5}$	0·2	$\frac{1}{100}$	0·01

Collins
New
Primary
Maths

Name _____ Date _____

Equivalent pizzas

● **Represent a problem by identifying the information
needed to solve it, find possible solutions and confirm
them in the context of the problem**

PIZZAS

Cheese and Tomato   buy it by the half
Vegetarian Feast   buy it in quarters
Mushroom   buy it in eighths
Hot pepperoni   buy it in sixths

Alexi buys $\frac{3}{4}$ of a pizza altogether.

What are the possible combinations of pizza he could have bought?

Show all your working.

Working out

Name _____ Date _____

Percentage problems

● **Understand percentage as the number of parts in every 100**

1   In Year 5 there are 30 children. 20% are absent. How many children is that?

2   There are 120 children. 75% of them want to go on a trip.
    There are 85 places. Can everyone go?

3   A test has 50 marks. Rory gets 40 marks. What is his percentage score?

4   Rick says that 3% is equivalent to $\frac{3}{10}$. Is he right? How do you know?

Collins New Primary Maths

Name _____ Date _____

Reviewing written multiplication and division

● **Use efficient written methods to multiply and divide HTU × U, TU × TU, U.t × U and HTU ÷ U**

For each calculation, approximate the answer first and write it in the bubble.

Then work out the answer. Show all your working.

a 642 × 6 ○ ○ ○

b 675 × 8 ○ ○ ○

c 765 × 7 ○ ○ ○

d 6·5 × 6 ○ ○ ○

e 8.4 × 5 ○ ○ ○

f 7.4 × 9 ○ ○ ○

g 67 × 95 ○ ○ ○

h 74 × 85 ○ ○ ○

i 92 × 46 ○ ○ ○

j 348 ÷ 6 ○ ○ ○

k 734 ÷ 5 ○ ○ ○

l 551 ÷ 9 ○ ○ ○

Name _____ Date _____

Number sequences

● Explain a generalised relationship in words

● Fill in the missing numbers in each sequence.
● Write the rule.
● Write the type of number sequence.

Combine two operations.

Add or subtract the same number each time.

Add the previous two numbers.

Add or subtract a changing number.

Multiply or divide the same number each time.

1 7, 14, 21, ____, ____, ____, ____, ____, 63

| The rule is |
| The type of number sequence is |

2 98, 102, 96, 104, 94, 106, ____, ____, ____

| The rule is |
| The type of number sequence is |

3 4, 40, 400, _____, _____, _____, 4 000 000

| The rule is |
| The type of number sequence is |

4 1, 2, 4, 7, 11, 16, ____, ____, ____, ____, 56

| The rule is |
| The type of number sequence is |

5 1, 4, 9, 16, ____, ____, ____, 64, ____, 100

| The rule is |
| The type of number sequence is |

6 5, 100, 20, 400, ____, ____, ____, ____, ____

| The rule is |
| The type of number sequence is |

Collins New Primary Maths